FIVE-STAR STAR

GIRLS' BASKETBALL DRILLS

Edited by Stephanie V. Gaitley

Wish
PUBLISHING

Wish Publishing
Terre Haute, Indiana
www.wishpublishing.com

Book edited by Stephanie V. Gaitley
Editorial consultation: Matt Masiero and Dave Odom
Proofread by Kim Heusel
Cover designed by Phil Velikan
Interior photographs provided by Justin Gracenin, Dave Odom and Five-Star Basketball Camp
Diagrams by Debbie Oldenburg

Printed in the United States of America
10 9 8 7 6 5 4 3 2 1

Published in the United States by
Wish Publishing
P.O. Box 10337
Terre Haute, IN 47801, USA
www.wishpublishing.com

Distributed in the United States by
Cardinal Publishers Group
Indianapolis, Indiana 46240

CONTENTS

Acknowledgments

Dear Coaches,

I want to thank everyone who participated in making this book come to life. The women's game will continue to grow because of our commitment to helping aspiring coaches learn more about the game through each other.

Thanks for taking the time out of your busy schedules to add your favorite drill or skill. I'm sure some young coaches will make great use of your information.

Best wishes for much continued success.

Sincerely,
Stephanie V. Gaitley,
Women's Basketball Coach,
St. Joseph's University

Introduction

Twenty years ago, Rick Pitino and Kathy Delaney-Smith put the idea of serious girls' basketball instruction the Five-Star way to work with the first-ever Five-Star Women's Camp at Boston University. Since that time, Five-Star has worked tirelessly to continue that idea with camps in seven states and clinics with the Turkish Basketball Federation that featured Wendy Larry of Old Dominion (1997) and Stephanie V. Gaitley of St. Joseph's University (1996). This book is a natural outgrowth of this philosophy.

Several thousand players have convened on our courts to take their game to the next level, whether that be making their high school team or playing in the WNBA. Players at every level of play can utilize the drills and philosophies found in this book. This book emphasizes what we teach at the Five-Star Camps: Success comes from the individual, her practice technique, her progressive goal planning and the intensity she brings to the court. With these three elements and a variety of creative drills for skill development, each player can become the best player she can be.

When *Five-Star Basketball Drills* was originally published in 1988, little did we know it was going to become the best-selling basketball drill book and inspire so many great players. To illustrate that point, when Trajan Langdon (currently of the Cleveland Cavaliers) was a senior in high school, he was asked how he had become such a great player. Trajan replied that he had studied a great deal of game tapes and that when he was a youth, his father had bought him a copy of the Five-Star drill book. He was so inspired that he used the book to practice two to three hours a day. We would like this book - filled with the best drills from today's top students of the game - to have the same influence on you, our reader, that the original *Five-Star Drills* had on Trajan and fill you with the determination and drill work you'll need to elevate your game.

We wish you the greatest success in your quest to achieve your potential.

Leigh Klein,
President of Five-Star International Basketball Camps

Matt Masiero,
Director, Five-Star Women's Camp

G. David Odom,
Director, Five-Star Women's Camp

CHAPTER ONE

Conditioning and Nutrition

Matt Brzycki, Coordinator of Health Fitness,
Strength and Conditioning Programs
Princeton University
Princeton, New Jersey

Strength & Conditioning

A strength-and-conditioning program is vital in preparing your athletes for the physical demands of basketball. There is, however, a wide range of programs from which to choose as well as considerable debate as to which one is most appropriate. As coaches, you are well aware that time is a precious commodity. Because of this, you should seek and implement a strength-and-conditioning program that produces the *maximum* results in the *minimum* amount of time. As such, efficiency should be the major consideration in selecting your program. By utilizing a program that is time-efficient, your athletes will have more time available to pursue other activities such as perfecting their basketball skills and preparing for academic experiences. Your players should *invest* time in a strength-and-conditioning program, not *spend* time.

STRENGTH TRAINING

The main purpose of strength training is to prevent injury. According to data collected for the NCAA Injury Surveillance System, the top two body parts that are most frequently injured in women's college basketball – in practices as well as games – have historically been the ankle and knee. Of particular concern are injuries to the anterior cruciate ligament (ACL) which occur in women basketball players seven times more frequently in practices and five times more frequently in games than in their male counterparts. Increasing the strength of your players' muscles, bones and connective tissue will allow them to tolerate stresses that might otherwise cause an injury.

A second purpose of strength training is to increase your players' performance potential. Strength training will not automatically make your athletes into better players but it will improve their *potential* to be better players. They must still learn how to apply their increased strength on the basketball court.

Interestingly, science has been unable to determine that one strength-training method is superior to another. Research has only shown that a variety of methods can increase strength. For example, one study found no statistically significant differences in the strength increases produced by nine different training routines consisting of various combinations of sets and repetitions. It has also been shown – both scientifically and empirically – that strength can be improved with a variety of equipment, including barbells, dumbbells and machines.

So, just about any type of strength-training program has the potential to produce favorable results. However, many methods of strength training are more favorable than others. For example, your strength-training program should be practical in the sense that it is relatively easy for you and your athletes to understand. In some instances, strength-training programs have become grossly overcomplicated and correspondingly confusing. The use of pseudoscientific terminology coupled with pre-planned programs that specify inflexible instructions to vary the sets, repetitions, intensity and volume of activity in rigidly defined "phases" of periodization adds to the confusion. Remember, too, that references to the training methodology of Eastern European weightlifters are irrelevant and, therefore, do not apply to your basketball players — unless your basketball players are also competitive weightlifters. And, of course, efficiency should be a major consideration.

A practical and efficient strength-training program can be designed — using virtually any type of equipment — by applying the following concepts:

Intensity

An athlete's level of intensity (or effort) is the most important factor in an efficient strength-training program. Essentially, the greater the intensity, the better the response. In the weight room, a high level of intensity is characterized by performing each exercise to the point of muscular fatigue: when an athlete has exhausted her muscles to the extent that she literally cannot perform any more repetitions. Failure to reach a desirable level of muscular fatigue — or effort — will result in submaximal gains in muscular strength.

Evidence for this "threshold" is suggested in the literature by the "Overload Principle" that was proven experimentally in the 1950s. The Overload Principle states that in order to increase muscular strength, a muscle must be stressed — or "overloaded" — with a workload that is beyond its present capacity. The effort must be great enough to exceed this threshold so that a sufficient amount of muscular fatigue is produced to trigger an increase in muscular strength. Simply, exercise that does not produce enough muscular fatigue will not stimulate muscular strength.

Progression

The term "Progressive Resistance Exercise" was coined in the 1940s. Unfortunately, little of what is done in most weight rooms today can be considered as being "progressive." Suppose that one of your athletes did a set of leg curls for 10 repetitions with 100 pounds and a month later she is still doing 10 repetitions with 100 pounds. Did she increase her strength? Probably not. On the other hand, what if she was able to do 11 repetitions with 120 pounds a month later? In this case, she performed 10 percent more repetitions with 20 percent more weight.

If a muscle is to continually improve in strength it must be forced to do progressively harder work. Muscles must be overloaded with a workload that is increased steadily and systematically throughout the course of a strength-training program.

The application of progression does not have to be as complex nor as restrictive as a periodization program. In order to overload her muscles, an athlete must attempt to increase either the weight that she used or the repetitions that she performed in relation to her previous workout. Each time an athlete achieves the maximum number of prescribed repetitions in an exercise, she should increase the resistance in that exercise for her next workout. The increase in resistance should be made in an amount with which each athlete is comfortable. Muscles will respond better if the progressions in resistance are five percent or less. But again, remember that the resistance must always be challenging.

If an athlete cannot do the maximum number of prescribed repetitions in an exercise, she should use the same resistance in that exercise for her next workout and try to perform a greater number of repetitions.

Sets

One of the most controversial areas in strength training concerns the number of sets that should be done for each exercise. For decades, it was generally accepted that performing multiple sets of an exercise was better than single sets. In 1998, Dr. Ralph Carpinelli and Dr. Robert Otto of Adelphi University (New York) destroyed this belief with an astonishing discovery. Their comprehensive literature review of all relevant research that examined different numbers of sets — 35 studies which dated back to 1956 — showed that there were no significant differences between single- and multiple-set training in all but two studies. In a later review, Dr. Carpinelli noted two additional studies that found no significant differences between single- and multiple-set training.

Besides the compelling scientific evidence, the fact of the matter is that performing one set to muscular fatigue is a very popular method of strength training. Indeed, single-set training is advocated by numerous strength-and-conditioning coaches at all levels of competition, including high school, college and professional.

If one set of each exercise produces the same results as two or three sets, then a one-set protocol represents a more efficient means of strength training. After all, why have your athletes perform several sets when they can obtain similar results from one set in a fraction of the time? This is not to say that traditional multiple-set programs are unproductive. It is just that multiple sets are extremely inefficient in terms of time and, therefore, are undesirable for your athletes.

Of course, if a single set of an exercise is to be productive, your players must do each exercise with an appropriate level of intensity — that is, to the point of muscular fatigue. Their muscle(s) must be completely fatigued at the end of each exercise.

Repetitions

In order to produce an increase in strength, a muscle must be exercised for an appropriate amount of time. Because it is characterized by short-term, high-intensity efforts, strength training is considered to be an anaerobic endeavor. Optimal time frames in the anaerobic domain are about 90 - 120 seconds for the buttocks, 60 - 90 seconds for the legs and 40 - 70 seconds for the upper torso.

This information can be used to formulate repetition ranges. For example, if a weight is raised in about two seconds and lowered in about four seconds, each repetition would be about six seconds long. Considering the aforementioned time frames and six-second repetitions yields the following repetition ranges: 15 – 20 for exercises involving the buttocks, 10 – 15 for the legs and 6 – 12 for the upper torso.

It should be noted that having your players attempt one-repetition maximums or perform low-repetition movements that are considerably less than the optimal time frames will increase their risk of injury. Likewise, as they exercise beyond the recommended time frames, it becomes a greater test of their aerobic endurance rather than anaerobic strength.

According to most authorities, strength training should not be done until the age of about 13 or 14. At this young age, it is safer to perform more repetitions than previously suggested in order to reduce orthopedic stress. The higher repetitions will necessitate using lighter weights that will, in turn, reduce the stress placed upon their bones and joints. For example, younger teenagers might use the following repetition ranges: 20 – 25 for exercises involving the buttocks, 15 – 20 for the legs and 10 – 15 for the upper torso.

Technique

Your athletes should raise the weight in a deliberate, controlled manner without any jerking movements. In general, they should raise the weight in about 1 – 2 seconds. Raising the weight in a rapid, explosive fashion is not recommended for two reasons. First, it increases the involvement of momentum thereby making the exercise less productive and less efficient; second, it exposes the muscles, joints and connective tissue to potentially dangerous forces which magnify the likelihood of incurring an injury while strength training.

After raising the weight, your athletes should pause briefly in the position of full muscular contraction or the "mid-range" position. Pausing momentarily in this position emphasizes their muscles when they are fully contracted. Further, a brief pause in the mid-range position permits a smooth transition between the raising and the lowering of the weight and helps reduce the adverse effects of momentum.

In order to attain optimal results from strength training, your athletes must emphasize the lowering of the weight. In general, they should lower the weight in about 3 – 4 seconds. Emphasizing the lowering of the weight makes the exercise more efficient: The same muscles that are used to raise the weight are also used to lower it. Therefore, each repetition becomes more efficient and each set becomes more productive.

In effect, each repetition should be roughly 4 – 6 seconds in length. A 16-week study demonstrated a 50 percent increase in upper-body strength and a 33 percent increase in lower-body strength in a group that performed each repetition by raising the weight in two seconds and lowering the weight in four seconds.

Finally, your athletes should perform each repetition throughout the greatest possible range of motion (ROM) that safety allows. Exercising throughout a full ROM will allow them to maintain — or perhaps increase — their flexibility. Furthermore, this ensures that the entire target muscle is being exercised — not just a portion of it — thereby making the movement more efficient. In other words, full-range exercise is necessary for a full-range effect.

Duration

More is not necessarily better when it comes to strength training (or conditioning, for that matter). Common sense suggests that as your athletes increase the length of their activity, they must decrease the level of their effort. Stated otherwise, your athletes cannot exercise with a high level of effort for long periods of time. Carbohydrates are the body's preferred source of energy during intense exercise. Most people exhaust their carbohydrate stores after about one hour of intense exercise. Therefore, strength workouts should be completed in no more than one hour — and even less when in-season.

Your athletes should take a minimum amount of recovery between exercises. The length of their recovery interval depends upon their present level of fitness. Initially, your athletes may require a recovery time of about three minutes between efforts; with improved fitness, their pace should be quickened to the point where they are moving as rapidly as possible between exercises. (The speed with which they perform their repetitions should not be quickened — just their pace between exercises.)

Volume

A strength-training program must address all of the major muscle groups in the body — not just the "showy" ones. Frequently, muscles that are injured while playing basketball get ignored (such as those surrounding the knee) while muscles that are more cosmetic than anything else get highlighted (such as the abdominals).

A comprehensive strength-training program for basketball can be performed using no more than 15 exercises during each total-body workout. The focal point for most of these exercises should be their hips, legs and upper torso. Specifically, one exercise should be included for their hips, hamstrings, quadriceps, calves/dorsi flexors, biceps, triceps, forearms, abdominals and lower back. Because the shoulder joint allows movement at many different angles, two exercises should be selected for their chest, upper back ("lats") and shoulders.

There is nothing wrong with having your athletes perform more movements than this in order to emphasize a particular body part. As long as they continue to make improvements in their strength, they are not doing too many exercises. However, if their strength begins to level off or "plateau" in one or more exercises, it is probably because they are overtraining. Along these lines, the volume of exercises should be reduced during the season.

Sequence

A strength-training program should begin with exercises that influence the largest muscles and proceed to those that involve the smallest muscles. Have your athletes perform exercises for their hips first, followed by their upper legs (hamstrings and quadriceps), lower legs (calves or dorsi flexors), upper torso (chest, upper back and shoulders), arms (biceps, triceps and forearms), abdominals and finally their lower back.

It is important that your athletes do not fatigue their midsection early in their workouts. The abdominals stabilize the rib cage and aid in forced expiration during intense activity. Therefore, early fatigue of their abdominals would detract from their performance in other exercises that involve their larger, more powerful muscles.

Frequency

Intense strength training places great demands on the muscular system. In order to adapt to those demands, your athletes must receive an adequate amount of recovery between strength workouts. Muscles do not get stronger during a workout — muscles get stronger during the recovery from a workout. When weights are lifted, muscle tissue is broken down and the recovery process allows the muscle time to rebuild itself. Think of this as allowing a wound to heal. If you had a scab and picked at it every day, you would delay the healing process. But if you left it alone, you would permit the damaged tissue time to heal. There are individual variations in recovery ability — everyone has different levels of tolerance for exercise. However, a period of about 48 - 72 hours is usually necessary for muscle tissue to recover sufficiently from an intense strength-training workout.

Adequate recovery is also required to return carbohydrate stores to their preexercise levels. Because approximately 48 hours are needed to replenish depleted carbohydrate stores following intense physical activity, it is suggested that your athletes perform their strength training 2 – 3 times per week on nonconsecutive days — such as on Monday, Wednesday and Friday.

Keep in mind that a strength-training program should be done year-round — including the basketball season. Remember, it is during the competitive season that your players need to be at their best in terms of strength (and conditioning). To provide adequate recovery, however, the frequency of their strength training should be reduced to 1 – 2 times per week when in-season.

Documentation

The importance of accurate record keeping cannot be overemphasized. Records are a log of what your athletes accomplish during each and every exercise of each and every workout.

A workout card can be an extremely valuable tool for you to monitor the progress of your athletes and make their workouts more meaningful. It can also be used to identify exercises in which an athlete has reached a plateau. In the unfortunate event that an athlete incurs an injury, the effectiveness of the rehabilitative process can be gauged if there is a record of her preinjury strength levels.

A workout card can take an infinite number of appearances. However, your athletes should be able to record their body weight, the date of each workout, the weight used for each exercise, the number of repetitions performed for each exercise and the order in which the exercises were completed. The recommended repetition ranges should also be given for each exercise along with spaces to record any seat adjustments.

CONDITIONING

In order for your basketball players to compete at their full potential, it is also important for them to be as highly conditioned as possible. Basketball — like most team sports — has an *anaerobic* element since it primarily consists of a series of short-term, high-intensity efforts. However, basketball also has an *aerobic* (or endurance) element since these anaerobic efforts are required over a fairly lengthy period of time. Conditioning for basketball, therefore, must involve aerobic and anaerobic efforts.

Similar to strength training, conditioning can be improved using a wide variety of equipment, including stationary bicycles, rowers and stairclimbers. Because basketball is a sport in which your athletes must run, most of their conditioning work should be accomplished by running. If you have heavier athletes, however, it is a good idea for them to do at least some of their conditioning with low-impact, nonweightbearing activities — such as pedaling stationary bicycles — to reduce the potential for orthopedic problems that can result from the high-impact forces of running.

You can design a practical and efficient conditioning program for your athletes by incorporating the following concepts:

Frequency

When not in-season, your players should do conditioning workouts three times per week on nonconsecutive days. It is critical to first establish a solid foundation of aerobic support. In the early off-season, then, these three workouts should be aerobic in nature — that is, they should consist of continuous, long-term efforts.

In the middle of the off-season, you should reduce the frequency of their aerobic workouts to twice a week and add an anaerobic workout in its place — such as interval training that involves repeated bouts of short-term, high-intensity efforts alternated with periods of recovery. At this point in the off-season, each of these efforts (sprints) should last about 1½ – 3 minutes. As an example, you might have your athletes run a series of four half-mile "intervals" with a goal of three minutes per interval.

By the end of the off-season, you should decrease their aerobic workouts to once a week and increase their anaerobic workouts to twice a week. At this point in the off-season, one of their anaerobic workouts should involve a series of "longer" efforts of 1½ - 3 minutes and the other a series of "shorter" efforts of less than 90 seconds.

During the preseason and in-season, most of your team's conditioning work can be done during practice. You can also have your players do different sprint drills at the end of practice.

Duration

Similar to strength training, more is not necessarily better when it comes to conditioning. Excluding a warm-up, conditioning workouts — whether they are aerobic or anaerobic — need not exceed 30 minutes. In fact, some conditioning workouts can be completed in as little as 18 - 20 minutes. Keep in mind, however, that although the length of the workout is low, the intensity of the effort that would be expected of your players is quite high.

Progression

Like strength training, it is important that conditioning be progressively more challenging. In general, there are three ways that your players can provide progression from one conditioning workout to the next. One way is to cover the same distance at a faster pace — that is, in a shorter amount of time. A second way is to cover a greater distance at the same pace. A third way is to increase both the distance and the pace.

In an aerobic workout in the early off-season, for example, you might require your players to run 3.00 miles in 24:00 (i.e., 24 minutes). To make the next aerobic workout more demanding, they could run 3.00 miles in 23:55, run 3.05 miles in 24:00 or 3.05 miles in 23:55. Anaerobic workouts should also be made progressively more challenging using similar methods.

YOUR DECISION

Coaches and players are quick to jump on the bandwagon of successful teams. In most cases, you will find that many teams are successful in basketball despite the fact that they use vastly different strength-and-conditioning programs. So, how do you decide on which program to

11

administer to your players? When you consider a strength-and-conditioning program, ask yourself the following five questions:

Is it productive?

Is it comprehensive?

Is it practical?

Is it efficient?

Is it safe?

If the answer to any one of these five questions is "no," then the program is not in the best interests of you or your players. Expressed in different terms, you should select and implement a program that is productive, comprehensive, practical, efficient and safe.

NOTE: This chapter represents a thumbnail overview of strength and conditioning for basketball. A more detailed description can be found in the book *Conditioning for Basketball* written by Matt Brzycki and Shaun Brown (the strength and conditioning coach of the Boston Celtics).

Debra Wein, M.S., R.D.
President and Co-Founder,
The Sensible Nutrition Connection
www.sensiblenutrition.com

Nutrition for Peak Performance

The body requires over 40 fundamental nutrients to maintain good health. To get all these nutrients and nonnutrient compounds important for health, it is best to eat a variety of foods from all food groups. No one food can supply your body with all the nutrients you need. Eating a diet that includes many different foods ensures you will get more of the vitamins, minerals and other substances your body needs to function its best and fight off disease. While some people think they can take a supplement to make up for a poor diet, many more substances in food are being discovered that may protect health and prevent disease. Therefore, be sure to include foods that contain all of the nuts and bolts your body needs for optimal health.

Have you ever wondered?

- What do fruits and vegetables have that milk doesn't?
- What's in lean meats that is not in pasta?
- What do the nutrients in the foods we eat every day do for us?

Check out the table on the following page to find out answers to these and other interesting questions.

Nutrient	Food Sources	What is it for?	How much do we need?
Carbohydrates	Breads, pasta, cereal, rice, grains, fruits, vegetables	Fuels the brain and muscles. The primary energy source for moderate-to-high intensity exercise.	55-65% of total calories The major source of calories in the diet.
Protein	meat, fish, eggs, poultry, beans, legumes, dairy	Essential for building and repairing every cell in the body. Not an optimal energy souce for exercise.	15-20% of total calories Requirements are easily met through food sources.
Fat	butter, oils, lard, margarine, salad, dressing, fried foods, mayo, shortening	Provides insulation and protection. The primary source of stored energy. Used for low-to-moderate intensity exercise. Source of essential fatty acids.	20-30% of total calories Most people get more than they need. Fat should be limited in individuals trying to lose weight.
Vitamins: water soluble & fat soluble	Eating a wide variety of foods will help you meet the RDAs for each vitamin	Metabolic *catalysts* that regulate reactions in the body. Your body cannot manufacture them - they must be obtained from food.	A Recommended Dietary Allowance (RDA) has been set for each essential vitamin at a safe and adequate level. RDAs are based on sex and age.

Nutrient	Food Sources	What is it for?	How much do we need?
Minerals	Eating a wide variety of foods will help you meet the RDAs for each mineral	Elements which combine to form structures of the body. Regulates body processes. Your body cannot manufacture them - they must be obtained from food.	A Recommeded Dietary Allowance (RDA) has been set for most essential minerals at a safe and adequate level.
Water	Beverages, fruits and vegetables	Essential substance making up 50-55% of your body weight. Transports nutrients and wastes in the body. Necessary for proper cell function.	Adequate amounts are necessary to replace daily loses.
Phytochemicals	Plant foods, especially fruits and vegetables	Nonnutrient substances which impart protective benefits to health. May Sbe important for reducing risk of cancer, heart disease, diabetes, cataracts & macular degeneration.	Choosing a minimun of five servings of fruits and vegetables daily may help reduce risk of many chronic diesases.

Identify Areas of Importance in the Diet

When examining your dietary intake, there are several areas of concern: quantity of food, quality of food, frequency of intake, and dietary behaviors. Although it is difficult to assess all areas at once, understanding the interaction between the areas over time will help you choose a diet:

1) Specific to your needs
2) Achievable for you
3) Compatible with the your lifestyle
3) Sustainable over the longterm

Quantity of food

Clearly overall calories are an important element. An estimate of the daily energy intake will allow for comparisons with daily energy expenditure and appropriate weight loss, gain, or maintenance. Moderate increases or decreases in daily intake, or levels of exercise over a period of time will produce permanent results – not drastic changes in calories.

Quality of food

Be sure to include regular and daily intake from all of the food groups. Consume a regular intake of bread, cereal, rice, pasta, fruit, vegetable, protein (fish, poultry, meat, legumes, soy products), and dairy.

Include a variety of:

♦ Bread and cereal - wheat, oat, multigrain, high fiber
♦ Rice - Brown, wild, basmati
♦ Pasta - whole wheat, spinach, various shapes and sizes
♦ Fruit - citrus, apples, pears, bananas, berries, melon
♦ Vegetable - cruciferous (broccoli, cauliflower, cabbage), dark leafy greens, squash, tomatoes, carrots
♦ Dairy - low-fat milk, yogurt, cheese

Choose fresh food

Processed foods are generally high in sodium and contain additives and preservatives, damaging flavor and nutrient content. Recently, new nutrients, termed phytochemicals (phyto meaning plants) were discovered in foods that provide our bodies with disease-preventing nutrients. Watch your vitamin and mineral supplement intake

Nutritional supplements continue to be very popular for a variety of reasons – their promise to provide things such as boosts in energy, weight loss, or increased performance. Take a look at the food you are eating versus the supplements you are taking. Are the supplements adding nutrients that otherwise would not be there or are they just adding excess energy to a diet that would benefit from a basic nutritional shape-up? A multi-vitamin/multi-mineral if you are trying to lose weight and extra carbs and adequate protein if you are in training are examples of beneficial supplementation; however, more often than not, supplementing to excess is the case. Sorting through the hype will save you effort and money.

Frequency of intake

1. Are your calories spread equally over the course of the day? A lot of people tend to eat light during the day and overeat at night. Starving during the day causes a drop in energy, often resulting in a search for a high-sugar snack. What you really need is to fuel your body over the day, especially if you are active. (The need to eat a lot at night will inevitably diminish over time in search of is energy.)
2. Is snacking being used healthfully or as a desperate attempt to get energy? Snacking can be the healthiest thing you do. Snacks can fill in the nutrient gaps in the overall diet. For example, if you rarely have milk or cheese in your meals and seem to be lacking dairy, try snacking on yogurt, frozen yogurt, or pudding (made with low-fat milk).
3. Are you a weekend eater? When the intake is "good" Monday through Friday afternoon and significantly different from Friday evening to Sunday, accomplishing goals is difficult. This is often a sign of severe restriction during the week that is leading to weekend binges.

Dietary behaviors

1. Do you eat in response to moods?
2. Which moods – anger, frustration, depression, or happiness?

3. Do you eat more when you are alone? When you are with others?
4. Do you plan ahead?
5. Are you in control of your environment or are you letting their environment control you?

Identifying negative behaviors is a good beginning, but it requires a lot of work and support to overcome them. Get additional help from a registered dietician and share your own experiences, if appropriate.

What does the extremely busy and active person need to know about nutrition? You can have a busy life and a healthy diet!

Do you feel like you are so busy that you barely have time to sleep, let alone eat healthy and exercise? We could all use an extra two (or more) hours in the day. Even though we know that fueling our bodies with healthy foods is very important, oftentimes our "life" gets in the way.

Does this sound familiar?

I'll start eating better...
> ...Next Monday
> ...After the big deadline
> ...When school is over
> ...When I have more time
> ...After the holidays

You barely have time to eat anything let alone think about eating healthy. Grocery shopping and preparing meals are often out of the question. The fact is that if you can't find the time...you MAKE the time! Your body will thank you in the long run! Contrary to popular belief (or popular excuses) eating a healthy diet is not "hard work." Like anything else, it just takes knowledge and practice. Below are some strategies to get you started. Remember, eating healthy is not all-or-nothing. Every positive change helps.

Suggestions For Fitting It All In When You Are On The Go

Plan. Plan what, when, where, and how. Schedule time to eat, just like you schedule a meeting. Busy lives mean planning and compromising. You can compromise on time without compromising on nutritional quality. Plan breakfast meetings, and develop a list of lunches and snacks you can eat at your desk or while you are on the go.

Eat a variety of foods that you like. Eating many different foods ensures that you get all the nutrients (and nonnutrient compounds) you need for optimal health without getting too many of the things that may not be as nutritious. Choosing a variety of foods also prevents boredom and increases the number of foods for you to choose from.

Snack. Snacking is also a great way to "take 5" and relieve stress. Always have nutritious snacks on hand to munch on. Choose nutrient-dense foods to fill in the gaps in your diet. If, for example, you have difficulty meeting your daily calcium requirements, choose yogurt, pudding, low-fat cheese or low-fat milk for snacking. Snacking helps you re-fuel and prevents you from becoming so hungry you overeat.

Be an Educated Eater. Learn the basics of good nutrition, label reading, and dining out. Being an Educated Eater means you have the knowledge necessary to make informed choices no matter how crunched for time you become.

Shop the perimeter of the grocery store. Think about where all the fresh food is usually located. Push your cart in a big circle and you will end up with a basket full of fresh fruits and vegetables just-baked whole-grain breads, low-fat dairy products, lean meats, poultry and fish. Go to the middle aisles for staples only. You'll save time and money.

Don't skip meals. Skipping meals not only causes you to miss nutrients important for you health and performance (mental and physical), it also can lead to overeating. You become so hungry that "anything goes" (into your mouth) and all good intentions go out the window. Oftentimes you end up eating the first thing you can grabthat may – or more likely may not – be nutritious, and lots of it.

Be creative. Think of time-saving eating opportunities such as eating while commuting, lunches you can eat at your desk, and dinners you can fix in 10 minutes or less. Keep in mind, dinner doesn't have to be hot to be nutritious and breakfast can be leftovers from a previous meal. Well-planned snacks can provide you with an opportunity to refuel and meet your nutritional requirements.

Be flexible. Things don't always work out the way we planned. Be prepared and have an alternative (or two). Don't give up or give in. Make the best of bad situations

Remember, you can fit good nutrition into a busy lifestyle if you...
-   -Make the commitment to your health
-   -Strive for improvements one at a time
-   -Set weekly goals
-   -Monitor your progress
-   -Reward your successes
-   -Be good to yourself
-   -Make healthy lifestyle changes
-   -Make the time

Depending on the duration, intensity and type of exercise you are performing, there are three stages where nutrition plays a role in performance – before, during and after activity. The goals of carbohydrate and fluid nutrition strategies are to optimize the availability of muscle glycogen and to keep the body well hydrated, thereby insuring optimal performance.

Preexercise nutrition
Properly nourishing yourself before exercise should:
-   ◆ Prevent low blood sugar during exercise
-   ◆ Provide fuel by topping off your muscle glycogen stores
-   ◆ Settle your stomach, absorb gastric juices and prevent hunger
-   ◆ Instill confidence in your abilities

Remember, fasting is detrimental to performance and is strongly discouraged before exercise or performance.

The preexercise meal should consist primarily of high-carbohydrate, low-fat foods for easy and fast digestion. Since everyone's preferences for, and responses to different foods are unique, it is recommended that you learn, through trial and error, what works and does not work for your own body. For example, some people respond negatively to sugar intake within an hour before exercise. The temporary "boost" that some people experience after eating foods with a high sugar (sucrose) concentration such as candy, syrups or soft drinks actually causes an increase in insulin production that will be followed by a rapid lowering of blood sugar and can lead to decreased performance. In addition, fructose (the sugar present in fruit juices) ingested before exercise may also lower your blood sugar and cause gastrointestinal distress in many people.

Allow adequate time for digestion and normalization of blood glucose:
- 4 hours for a large meal
- 2 - 3 hours for a smaller meal
- 1 hour for a blended meal, a high carbohydrate beverage (10-30%), or a small snack

For an early morning event, plan wisely so that you can consume at least a smaller meal 2-3 hours before race time. If you know you get nervous or jittery and lose your appetite before an event, make a special effort to eat well the day before. Always eat familiar foods before a competition, don't try anything new and risk affecting your performance. Experiment only during your training.

Foods high in carbohydrates include: fruits, cereal, pasta, breads, rice and other grains.

During exercise

When you eat a diet that is already high in carbohydrates, 60% or greater, there is enough energy in the muscles to fuel workouts and other activities completed within 90 - 120 minutes. On the other hand, during prolonged, strenuous exercise lasting over 2 hours, carbohydrate ingestion at regular intervals during the exercise is beneficial. For example, consuming 8 ounces (1 cup) of a sport drink containing a 6 - 10 % carbohydrate concentration every 15 - 20 minutes can delay the onset of fatigue. This is equivalent to a rate of .8 - 1.0 grams of carbohydrate per minute or approximately 24-30 grams every half hour.

Postexercise nutrition

When and what you eat after a workout can have a serious effect on your recovery. Adequate recovery means that your muscles are rested, refueled and ready to perform again, which is extremely important for people who exercise every day. Inadequate recovery can lead to chronic fatigue and a gradual decline in your performance. Be selective in what you eat after exercise; wise choices will help you recover quickly and enable your muscles to work better the next time around. For the fitness enthusiast whose workouts generally last less than 90 minutes, your main concern is to refuel with a well-balanced, high-carbohydrate diet. However, if your workouts typically last longer than 90 minutes and are "exhaustive," the timing of your meals is additionally important. Your body needs about 20 hours to replenish its fuel stores. Furthermore, this will only occur if adequate carbohydrates (approximately 500-600 grams depending on your body size) are consumed during this time. The first 2-3 hours after exercise are critical for you; don't wait to eat.

For optimal glycogen resynthesis follow these target intakes during the 20 hours following a workout:

- Immediately after exercise (15-30 minutes): 75-100 grams carbohydrate
- Within the next 2-3 hours after exercise: 100 grams carbohydrate
- Every 4 hours thereafter: 100 grams carbohydrate

For example, since 1 gram carbohydrate = 4 calories, 75-100 grams = 300 - 400 calories. In practical terms, you could take in 75-100 grams of carbohydrate by eating:

- A banana and a bagel
- 1/2 cup raisins and a slice of bread
- 2 cups of orange juice and a cup of yogurt.

A high-carbohydrate beverage (10-30% carbohydrate concentration) can also be used as an immediate source of carbohydrate replenishment. These beverages can be especially useful after a workout in the heat when you may be more inclined to drink than to eat. However, high carbohydrate beverages are not complete foods; they do not contain all the nutrients your body needs for good health and top performance. If you use these beverages in your training regimen, make sure you follow soon after with a well-balanced, high-carbohydrate meal and plenty of fluids.

Fluid and hydration guidelines

Water is an essential nutrient making up 50-55% of your weight. Water cools your body. As you exercise your body temperature increases and you sweat. As the sweat evaporates from your skin, you cool down. Dehydration will occur if the body water you lose is not replaced. You can become dehydrated even when you lose just a few pounds of water as sweat. Dehydration can be dangerous resulting in chills, clammy skin, throbbing heartbeat, nausea and decreased performance. Here's what you need to know to avoid dehydration!!!

Before exercise: *Hyper-hydrate*

Drink before exercise! 1-2 hours before exercise drink 2 1/2 cups (20 oz.) of water.

15-30 minutes before exercise drink another 1 1/2 cups (12 oz.) of water for a total of 4 cups (32 oz.).

During exercise: *Hydrate*

Drink 1 cup (8 oz.) of water or sport drink every 15-20 minutes during a workout.

After exercise: *Rehydrate*

Weigh yourself before and after a workout. For each pound of body weight lost drink 2 cups (16 oz.) of water or sport drink. If you don't have access to a scale, drink until your urine is clear. Clear urine is a good indication of adequate hydration.

Other tips to keep you performing at your best:

- Drink before you're thirsty since thirst is not always a good indicator of fluid loss.
- Avoid caffeine and alcohol, they increase fluid losses.
- Drink fluids at a cool temperature.
- Unless you are an ultraendurance athlete participating in events lasting over 8 hours, electrolyte (sodium, potassium, and chloride) losses from exercise are easily overcome by typical intakes from the regular diet. Therefore, salt tablets and other electrolyte replacements are not recommended.

Coach Cheryl Dozier
University at Buffalo
Buffalo, New York

10 Seconds

Purpose:
To improve transition, running the floor and conditioning skills.

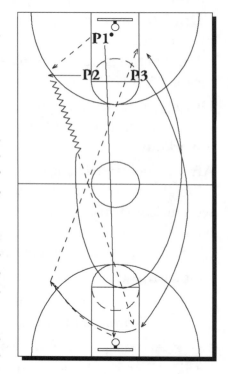

Organization:
This drill requires three players.

1) The drill begins with three players standing in the lane. Player 1 has the ball in front of the basket and the other two are at the elbows with at least one foot inside the paint.

2) Player 1 throws the ball off the glass, rebounds it, and outlets it to one of the other players who have gone to the outlet positions as the ball hits the glass.

3) The player who catches the outlet is to push the ball up the middle of the floor.

4) The player who does not receive the outlet will sprint up the floor and receive the long pass from the wing with the ball for a lay-up.

5) After passing for the lay-up, the player who makes the pass (player 2 in the diagram) has to touch one foot in the paint and sprint back the other way, this time to be the player who receives the pass and shoots the lay-up.

6) Player 1's job is to simply sprint the floor, take the ball out of the net, and outlet it to the player who hit the lay-up (player 3 in the diagram).

7) Player 3, after she makes her lay-up, sprints to the outlet position and will throw the long pass to player 1.

8) Not only must the two lay-ups be made in the allotted 10 seconds, but all three players must have a foot in the paint before 10 seconds are up as well.

Coach Matt Masiero
Director, Five-Star Women's Basketball Camp
Boston, Massachusetts

Agility Series

Purpose:
To improve footwork, quickness and agility.

Organization:
Each drill is done at full speed to maximize the benefits and simulate game conditioning.

A. Line Series
Each drill is done in 15-second intervals up to 1 minute.
For example: first set is 15 seconds, second set is 30 seconds and so on.
1. Player finds a line on the court (baseline, sideline or free-throw line) and begins to jump over the line a left to right, jumping with both feet together, knees bent and hands above the head.

2. Repeat Drill 1, but now jump forward and backward.

3. Repeat Drill 1 and 2, but incorporate them together to form a box. Example: forward, left, backward and right.

4. W-Form: Player uses the same form as in Drills 1-3, but now forms a W.

B. Minuteman/Lunge Series
1. Player finds a line on the court (baseline, sideline or free-throw line) and gets into a defensive stance. With the leg that is on

the line, the player pushes off using that leg and lunges forward with the opposite leg, pointing the toe in the direction of the lunge.

2. Repeats Drill 1, but increase to 2, 3 and 4 lunges consecutively.

3. Repeat Drill 1, but turn and face the opposite way using the opposite leg to push off on.

C. Ladder Drill

1. Player sprints 1 full length of court in 5 seconds.

2. 3 lengths in 15 seconds.

3. 5 lengths in 30 seconds.

4. 7 lengths in 40-45 seconds

5. 9 lengths in 55-60 seconds

6. 11 lengths in 65-70 seconds.

7. 13 lengths in 80-90 seconds.

8. 15 lengths in 95-105 seconds.

9. Repeat drill going down (15, 13, 11, 9, 7, 5, 3, and 1). Same times.

10. Allow equal time for sprint and then rest

Coach Keith Holubesko
Rogers High School
Newport, Rhode Island

Rope Burn

Purpose:
Skipping rope is one of the most efficient ways to condition the body. This drill also emphasizes foot speed, body coordination and lower leg strength.

Organization:
We have our players do this workout three times a week. It is important that the rope moves continuously.

Time	Rate	Foot Position
60 seconds	moderate	together
30 seconds	fast	alternate feet
60 seconds	moderate	together
60 seconds	fast	together
20 seconds	moderate	left leg only
20 seconds	moderate	right leg only
20 seconds	fast	left leg only
20 seconds	fast	right leg only
20 seconds	fast	together
60 seconds	moderate	together

Total Time: 6:10

Coach Bill Agronin
Niagara University
Niagara University, New York

Tip-N-Sprint

Purpose:
To develop teamwork, ball control and cardiovascular endurance.

Organization:
Players divide into two units with one unit at each end of the court. O1 and O2 tip the ball against the backboard simultaneously and sprint to the opposite end. O3 follows and mimics O1; O4 follows and apes O2. Play is continuous and lasts for a predetermined amount of time.

Coaching Points:
- Players must jump up and meet the ball.
- Players must not let the ball touch the floor.

Variations:
- If the task at hand is too difficult to youngsters, have them jump up, catch the ball, come down with it, then jump back up and shoot or toss it against the backboard.
- When a ball touches the floor, the time is started over.

Kevin L. Allen
West Florence High School
Florence, South Carolina

3-2-3 Conditioning Drill

Contributor's Note: I wish I could take full credit for this drill but I got this from Susan Walvius at South Carolina.

This is a great conditioning drill that employs sprinting, turning, change of direction. In my practice I usually divide my team into posts and guard groups. Each group will run the drill seperately. Time is put on the clock.

This can vary but I use 3:00 minutes as did USC. Players will first run 3 down-and-back sprints, hence the first "3." After the completion of the sprints they will run from baseline to free-throw line. Once the reach the free-throw line they will turn and backpedal until they reach the other free throw line in which they will turn and sprint to the end line. After reaching the end line they will sprint forward to the free throw line, turn and backpedal until they reach the other free-throw line then sprint forward. This continues two times, hence the "2". They will then run 3 down-and-back sprints for the final "3". This is a continuous running drill. They have 3 minutes to complete the drill.

Coach Kathy Warner Corbett
Oglethorpe University
Atlanta, Georgia

Conditioning Full-court Drills

Purpose: To warmup team and improve overall conditioning.

Organization:

1) *Full-court Lay-ups.* Must make 90 lay-ups in two minutes. Players shoot first with right hand, then left hand. Coaches count made lay-ups (see diagram 1).

2) *Three Line Shooting.* Three players pass to halfcourt. Middle person takes a lay-up. Outside people get a pass from the baseline for a jump shot. Three people on the baseline go for a continuous drll (see diagram 2).

Diagram 1   Diagram 2

Coach Eric Stratman
Quincy Senior High School
Quincy, Illinois

Group Exercises & Conditioning

Purpose:
To get the team warmedup and ready to go at the beginning of every practice.

Organization:
1) *Fingertip Pushups:* Squad starts flat on floor; on whistle, they push up on fingertips until next whistle (usually 10 seconds). They then do 10 or more of these at their own pace and this is followed by 10 more normal pushups using the palms of the hands.

2) *Arch Lifts:* Squad stands flat-footed; on whistle, each player springs from bent knees as high as she can and lands on her toes. Immediately, with arms fully extended above her head, she then jumps as high as she can without bending her knees (only from and onto her toes) 20 times. This whole process is repeated four more times.

    Then each girl, starting flat-footed, bounces up and down on her toes 20 times. She does a series of five of these.

    A stretching, even a painful sensation, will be felt in the gastroenemius muscles and in the Achilles tendons when this drill is done correctly and completely.

3) *Ankle Walk:* Squad, in single file, walks the baseline on the outside of their ankles, turns at the sideline and walks on the insides of their ankles, turn at the 10-second line and walk on the tip toes across the 10-second line and turn and come down the other sideline on the heels. Emphasis on the stretching and working of muscles, tendons and ligaments of the ankle joint.

4) *Bankboard Tipping:* Squad lines up in a single-file line. Lead player puts a ball up against the board. The next player steps forward, leaps catches ball with arms extended and, at the top of her jump, rebounds the ball back up against the board using only her fingers and wrists (see diagram 1).

Diagram 1

Next woman gets the rebound and repeats. After tipping, a player runs around the coach and back to the end of the line.

A goal is set (100, etc.) before the drill is started and the drill continues until that many in a row are tipped correctly and the last one is made.

By stepping one step backward after each tip, the coach can bring about much running between tips and less standing around.

Variations:

♦ Have another ball going at the same time at the basket at the other end. A player must run to the other end after her turn at one end.

♦ Have two lines going at once at one basket.

♦ Have each player tip three or four times straight when it is her turn.

♦ After tipping, the player crosses the lane and the ball is tipped by the next player across the rim to her. She tips the ball back across the rim to the next player and then goes to the end of the line.

5) *Run-Shuffle Drill:* Players (spaced) run hard from court corner to free throw line extended. Each plants her outside foot and makes abrupt change here to good defensive shuffle step across floor.

At the sideline, players plant their outside foot and make abrupt change to hard run to 10-second line and then shuffle across the floor to the sideline. Forward run to free-throw line extended, shuffle across, forward to baseline, and shuffle across end. This is one trip, and the squad continues until five complete, perfect trips are made by all (see diagram 2).

6) *Rope Jumping:* Often, half of our squad is doing the rope jumping while the other half is doing the next drill (the block drill). They take about the same amount of time and the two groups can thus trade off equipment when they finish.

Diagram 2

♦ For one minute: jump with both feet.

♦ For one minute: jump with right foot only.

♦ For one minute: jump with left foot only.

♦ For one minute: jump by alternating feet.

Variations:

♦ Jump 20 times each with both, right, left, alternate and then start the series again and continue until the four minutes are up.

♦ Add tricks, such as:
  - double jumps (rope passes under feet twice in one jump)
  - crossed arms
  - backward jumping
  - boxer shuffle
  - rope folded in half
  - rope folded in quarters

7) *Block Drill:* Each player was three blocks. Blocks are made of wood and measure 2" x 3" x 4". Half the squad lines up behind one another down the middle of the lane. One block is in the each player's hand, one is just outside the right lane line and the third is outside the left

lane line. On the coach's whistle, the players all slide to the left with a good defensive slide and head up and exchange blocks with one on the floor. They then slide back to the right, then the left, then the right, etc. Players go hard for one minute, then rest for 15 seconds. Repeat twice.

Variations:
- Two sets of 90 seconds.

- Three sets of 30 seconds *done twice as fast as normal.*

8) *Stairs:* Self-explanatory. Players must be watched to make sure each step is struck and that only the front part (the ball) of the foot is used.

9) *Barrier Jumping:* A subsitute for the old standard bench jumping. Barriers made of electrical conduit (it bends) set in 20" long 2 x 4 bases. (As an alternative, jump ropes are held by two players and jumped by a third can work as well)

Two sets of 18 jumps the first night and increase by one each practice until players are doing two sets of 36. There is to be no little jump between jumps as there often is in rope jumping, it's jump-jump-jump-jump-jump, etc.

10) *Apache Drill:* One-half of squad lines up along the basline; on whistle, players sprint full speed to free-throw line extended and change direction; run backward to baseline and change again. They run forward to the 10-second line, backward to the baseline, forward to far free-throw line extended, backward back to baseline, forward to opposite end line, backward to base.

Then they work their way back the same way, hitting the free throw line, the 10-second line and, finally, the near free-throw line again. At each line, every player must pat both hands on the floor beyond the line. Each player goes twice to complete the drill.

Variations:
- Use clock and compete juniors vs. seniors, tall vs. short, etc. Winner gets out of running the drill the second time.

- Late-season variation: have squad send one player to free-throw line. If she can make eight out of 10, the whole squad can skip this drill.

11) *Long Lay-up Drill:* The players line up in two lines at the end line, facing downcourt. Each player in left line has a ball. Each pair can use just three passes to go the full length of the court for a lay-up. There is no chance of not going full speed.

At varsity level, drill will stop when no mistakes in passing, footwork or lay-up shooting occurs during one complete squad trip. Lower levels adjust on number of passes allowed and acceptable percentage (see diagram 3).

12) *Super Rebounder Drills:* Player starts along the lane and throws the ball up gainst the bankboard across the rim. She quickly crosses the lane and catches the ball. Her feet must both be outside the lane for the try to "count. " Players go for one minute, or 25 "good ones," whichever comes first.

This is an excellent drill to emphasize that a good rebounder does not have to have the ball come to her side (see diagram 4).

Diagram 3

Diagram 4

Coach Craig Kennedy
Auburn University
Auburn, Alabama

Crosscourt Conditioning

Purpose:
To improve overall conditioning, ballhandling skills and setting screens.

Organization:
This conditioning drill goes the width of the court. Make sure players touch the lines, stop and set good screens with hand signals and call their partner's name. Focus on execution when tired. Players can have water bottles at the end of their line to ensure that they stay hydrated if you wish. Always time this exercise to keep players putting forth maximum effort each time. Make sure everyone stays to encourage teammates to finish strong.

1) Put your team into groups of two or three on the sideline.

2) The first person in each line has a ball.

3) Dribble left-handed to the opposite sideline. Touch the sideline with a foot and return with the opposite hand. Do this three times.

4) Pass the ball when about five feet away and then set a screen for your partner.

5) Partner drives tight off the shoulder and dribbles left-handed to the other side.

6) Each group follows these repetitions. Three sets of "there and back" with the ball, pass and screen. One set of there and back, pass and screen. Three sets of there and back without a ball, tag off with your partner. Two sets of there and back without the ball, tag off with your partner. One set of there and back. On the last set, have athletes execute defensive footwork (slide) there and back, and then tag off.

Options include dribbling forward and backward, two-sball dribbling and increasing the number of repititions of defensive footwork.

Coach Bob Starkman
Broward Community College
Miami, Florida

Overall Conditioning Drills

Purpose:
To develop overall team conditioning.

Diagram 1

Organization:

1) *Pass and Attack.* Two lines form on each baseline. Line one passes the ball to line two. After pass, the players from line one sprint to defend the shot. Line two (the shooters) catch the ball and quick release a jumper. Players switch lines and repeat (see diagram 1).

2) *Stress Shooting.* Player simulates five jump shots. On her sixth shot, the player releases and shoots the jump shot. Continue each various area until 10 shots are made.

3) *Sit-ups while Dribbling.* Players sit on floor with their knees up. They begin to do sit-ups while dribbling basketball. Start with 25 on each side and increase each day.

4) *Key Pickup.* Players line up in a defensive position. Place a set of keys on foul line. Elbow player must defensive slide, pickup keys, and place them down. Repeat for one minute.

5) *Foul-line Lay-up.* For one minute, player shoots continous lay-ups. Players move from foul line back. Only one dribble allowed on lay-up. Players keep count of their lay-ups.

Diagram 2

6) *Nine Drill*. Players line up: three up, three down and three waiting. Three players bring ball up and play against the three waiting. Once the waiting three have possession of the ball, they become the offense and go downcourt and play against the three waiting there. Players continue to repeat the process (see diagram 2).

7) *Nutsy Drill*. Players form two lines. One passes (chest), the other passes (bounce). Players go up- and downcourt doing this; they must slide up- and downcourt while passing the ball.

Coach Bob Starkman
Broward Community College
Miami, Florida

Rock Drill

Purpose:
To develop overall team conditioning, rebounding, passing and shooting

Organization:
Players divide into two lines: one at half-court and one under the basket. The player under the basket jumps 10 times, as high as she can off glass (simulating rebounding off glass). On the 10th jump, the player at half-court sprints to center half-court area (jump ball area) and yells, "outlet." The player receives the "outlet" pass and fast breaks toward the opposite basket. At this time,

the player who threw the outlet pass sprints down the side. The player that received the pass stops at the foul line and hits original player with a bounce pass and lays it in. Continue drill while each player rotates lines.

Scenes from Five-Star

CHAPTER TWO

Ballhandling Drills

Coach Amy Meehan
Drury High School
North Adams, Massachusetts

Points in Ballhandling

Purpose: Listed below are points of concern which should be kept in mind when working on a player's ballhandling skills

1. Thirty-second reps of ballhandling drills build confidence handling the ball and acts as a good warm-up.
2. Practice ballhandling routines daily.
3. Always keep head up.
4. Be sure to concentrate on fingertip control when handling the ball.
5. Movement should be clockwise and counterclockwise.
6. Work on minimizing fumbles as you become more advanced.

Why utilize the dribble?
   a. Advance the ball up the floor.
   b. Get ball closer to the basket.
   c. Improve a passing angle.
   d. Get out of trouble.

Points of Emphasis:
   a. Don't waste your dribble; dribble with a purpose.
   b. See entire floor when you dribble.
   c. Only pick up dribble to pass or shoot.

Drills for Ballhandling

Purpose: Emphasize the importance of getting into a routine and working on it daily, with both the right and left hand. Ballhandling/dribbling drills focus on the following five aspects: control, speed, spin movement, change of pace and change of direction

Organization:
1) Warm-up Routine (each player must have a ball)
   a) *Ball Slaps*. Players should slap ball with both hands, get a feel for the ball.
   b) *Fingertips*. Players should extend arms straight up over head, shoulder-width apart. Players should move ball from right to left over their head using their fingertips. After a few seconds, have players move arms straight and move ball right to left in front of their chests.
   c) *Around the World*. Players should circle body with ball around waist, knees and ankles. Be sure to go in both right and left directions.
   d) *Leg Circles*. Single leg circles around each leg, in both directions.
   e) *Figure Eights*. Players should be in a comfortable stance, making a figure eight movement with the ball between their legs.
   f) *Figure Eight Dribble*. Same as above, but players dribble in a figure eight, both hands in both directions.
   g) *Ball Catch*. Players stand shoulder-width apart, knees bent, holding the ball between their legs. Players should alternate catching ball front to back, back to front.
   h) *Dribble Circle*. Sitting on the floor, player puts legs and feet together with the knees slightly bent. Dribble ball in circle around legs with both right and left. Dribble around legs only — not 360 degrees around body.
   i) *Whirl*. Same as above but continue around entire body.
   j) *Sleeper*. Lie down, dribble with the right hand. On coach's command, players sit up and bring ball under their legs to their left hand. Lie down, continue dribbling and repeat.

2) Wall Dribble: Line players up against the wall. Have players dribble with right hand against the wall, using finger tips and keeping ball in control. On command have players crossover dribble from their right hand to their left hand. Alternate right and left, always using the crossover to switch hands.

3) Individual Dribble Moves
   a) *Crossover*. Line players up on endline. On whistle, players dribble at a comfortable pace. Emphasize control versus speed. On double whistle, players should cross ball over to other hand on court.

b) *Hesitation.* This dribble move should emphasize a change of pace or a "hesitation" or "stutter step." Use hesitation to bring defender close in on offense; player should explode by defender.

c) *Spin Dribble.* This dribble move allows player to change her direction and seal off her defender. Player dribbles on a diagonal, keeping ball on outside hip. Continue to dribble and plant the foot farthest from the ball. This foot becomes the pivot foot. Next, reverse pivot by dropping the nonpivot foot. As this "spin" is being made the ball should be switched to the other hand, which allows the ball handler to continue protecting to the ball on the outside hip as the direction has been changed. Continue dribble and alternate spin dribble moves.

Coach Duffy Burns
Cleveland State University
Cleveland, Ohio

The Daily Dozen

Diagram 1

Diagram 2

Diagram 3

Purpose:
To improve game conditioning, ballhandling and shooting.

Organization:
1) Underhand Lay-up (See Diagram 1)
   a) Dribble right
   b) Plant with left foot
   c) Shoot right

Diagram 4

2) Overhand Lay-up (See Diagram 2)
   a) Dribble right
   b) Plant with left foot
   c) Shoot right

3) Under Same Hand (See Diagram 3)
   a) Dribble right
   b) Plant with left foot
   c) Shoot right

Diagram 5

Diagram 6

Diagram 7

Diagram 8

Diagram 9

Diagram 10

Diagram 11

4) Under Opposite Hand (See Diagram 4)
   a) Dribble right
   b) Plant with right foot
   c) Shoot left

5) Slide (See Diagram 5)
   a) Dribble right
   b) Jump stop
   c) Shoot right or left

6) Roll Hook (See Diagram 6)
   a) Dribble left
   b) Plant with right foot
   c) Shoot left

7) Underhand Lay-up (See Diagram 7)
   a) Dribble left
   b) Plant with right foot
   c) Shoot left

8) Overhand Lay-up (See Diagram 8)
   a) Dribble left
   b) Plant with right foot
   c) Shoot left

9) Underhand Same Hand (See Diagram 9)
   a) Dribble left
   b) Plant with right foot
   c) Shoot left

10) Under Opposite Hand (See Diagram 10)
    a) Dribble left
    b) Plant with right foot
    c) Shoot right

11) Slide (See Diagram 11)
    a) Dribble left
    b) Jump stop
    c) Shoot right or left

Diagram 12

12) Roll Hook (See Diagram 12)
    a) Dribble right
    b) Plant with left foot
    c) Shoot right

Coach Duffy Burns
Cleveland State University
Cleveland, Ohio

Daily Dozen II

Diagram 1

Diagram 2

Diagram 3

Diagram 4

Diagram 5

Purpose:
To improve game conditioning, ballhandling and shooting.

Organization:
1) Lateral Cross (See Diagram 1)
   a) Dribble right
   b) Jump stop
   c) Plant with right foot
   c) Shoot left

2) Diagonal Cross (See Diagram 2)
   a) Dribble right
   b) Jump stop
   c) Plant with right foot
   d) Shoot left

3) Step Around (See Diagram 3)
   a) Dribble right
   b) Jump stop

Diagram 6　　　　　*Diagram 7*　　　　　*Diagram 8*

    c) Plant with left foot
    d) Shoot jumper

4) Glide (See Diagram 4)
    a) Dribble left
    b) Jump stop
    c) Shoot right

5) Runner (See Diagram 5)
    a) Dribble left
    b) Plant with right foot
    c) Shoot jumper

6) Jump Hook (See Diagram 6)
    a) Dribble right – back player into block
    b) Plant with right foot
    c) Shoot left

7) Lateral Cross (See Diagram 7)
    a) Dribble left
    b) Jump stop
    c) Plant with left foot
    c) Shoot right

8) Diagonal Cross (See Diagram 8)
    a) Dribble left
    b) Jump Stop
    c) Plant with left foot
    d) Shoot right

Diagram 9

Diagram 10

Diagram 11

Diagram 12

9) Step Through (See Diagram 9)
   a) Dribble left
   b) Jump Stop
   c) Plant with right foot
   d) Shoot jumper

10) Glide (See Diagram 10)
    a) Dribble right
    b) Jump stop
    c) Shoot left

11) Runner (See Diagram 11)
    a) Dribble right
    b) Plant with left foot
    c) Shoot jumper

12) Jump Hook (See Diagram 12)
    a) Dribble left – Back player into block
    b) Plant with left foot
    c) Shoot right

Coach Nelson Schorr
SUNY Potsdam
Potsdam, New York

Change-of-Direction Drill

Purpose:
To improve ballhandling, change of direction, individual moves and help-side defense.

Organization:

1) Offensive player starts out on the wing, one step out from the three-point line. Two defenders are playing defense. One of them is coming from the elbow and the other will come from the help side.

Diagram 1: Defender stops in the middle, reverses, and changes direc-

2) The offensive player takes one dribble toward the elbow defender who tries to stop her from going to the middle.

3) The offensive player then changes direction on the dribble and starts to go to the baseline.

4) The weakside defender comes from the lane and stops the offensive player from getting to the baseline.

Diagram 2: Defender stops at the baseline. Offensive player changes direction and goes to the middle.

5) The offensive player then changes direction on the dribble again and goes into the lane to shoot a short jump shot.

Diagram 3: *Offensive player goes to the middle.*

Coaching Points:

♦ The offensive player uses three dribbles to accomplish the drill. The players would then rotate and go the other side of the floor and do the drill again.

Coach Kathy Warner Corbett
Oglethorpe University
Atlanta, Georgia

Dribble Drills

Purpose: To improve ballhandling.

Dribble Tag
Organization:
1) Each player starts with a basketball. They begin dribbling on the whistle and must continue dribbling while trying to knock balls away from the others.

2) If a player picks up the ball or double dribbles, she is out and must take the ball and sit on the sideline.

3) If a player steps out of bounds, she is out (set boundaries depending on your number of players — half of the court is usually effective).

4) As the game continues and more people get out, the boundaries will need to be made smaller.

5) Play continues until you have one winner.

Two-Ball Drag Dribble
Organization:
1) With a ball in each hand, players walk slowly backward *dragging* balls in front of them. Keep the ball very low to the ground, use only fingertips and keep elbows completely straight. Players do this until they reach halfcourt.

2) Players walk forward from halfcourt, dragging the balls just behind each ankle very low to the ground (make sure they keep ball *behind* ankle).

Two-Ball Dribble Figure Eight

Organization:

1) With one ball in the right and one ball in the left hand, drag the ball in left hand around left leg. Keep ball very low to the ground using only fingertips while continuing to dribble the ball in right hand off to the right side (very low to the ground). Continue the process with the other hand. Do not cross balls from right hand to left hand.

Coach Jack Miller
Rider University
Lawrenceville, New Jersey

Ballhandling Movement Drills

Purpose: To improve ballhandling skills

Organization:

1) Right hand controlled full court with three dribbles and explode by the defender or cone at free-throw line/halfcourt/free-throw line/ end line. Jump stop and switch to left hand and repeat (20 seconds total, 10 seconds down and 10 seconds back).

2) Right hand on side, perform a protected inside-out dribble on same side of body with same hand to free-throw line/halfcourt/free-throw line/end line. Then switch to left hand after jump stop and continue (20 seconds total, 10 seconds down and 10 seconds back).

3) Dribble drive, double crossover fast and strong at all divisions on the court. Same coming back (20 seconds).

4) Pullback, crossover move. Take two dribbles back out of trap and then explode into a crossover dribble (20 seconds total, 10 seconds down and 10 seconds back).

5) Hesitation move, shuffle at defender/cone, then take a big step by while changing pace with crossover dribble (20 seconds total, 10 seconds down and 10 seconds back).

6) Between the legs at each line. Single going down and double going back (20 seconds).

7) Speed dribbling into jump stop, reverse pivot on end lines going down and back, right and left hand (20 seconds).

8) Cooldown (40 seconds.)

Total Workout Time: 10 minutes.

Coach Eric Stratman
Quincy Senior High School
Quincy, Illinois

Group Ballhandling Drills

Purpose:
To improve overall ballhandling and passing skills.

Organization:

Diagram 1

1) *Heads-Up Drill:* First player in each line has a ball. The coach signals movement of dribbling with hand. Players have to keep their head up and dribble at the same time (see diagram 1). This is an excellent drill with younger players and can be used for defensive slide work and conditioning also. Delays can be designed and used when players are executing the drill.

This drill also provides an excellent opportunity to practice pivot footwork. Front player can dribble out, stop, pivot and return to pass to the next player in line. All four pivots should be practiced: forward right, forward left, reverse right and reverse left.

2) *Peripheral Vision Drill:* Two balls are used. Player in middle keeps one ball going back and forth between herself and end player (see diagram 2).

The other ball is kept moving up and down between the middle player, the next player in line, the next, etc.

Diagram 2

3) *Bull-in-the-Ring:* Good drill for passing under pressure and, if you have a larger group

of players, for practicing passing while being two-timed.

Player in ring must try to touch the ball as the other players pass it around. Passer can not pass to a player right next to her. If the player in the middle touches the ball, the player who is responsible for this is then put in the center (see diagram 3). With a very large group, put two or three players in the ring at one time.

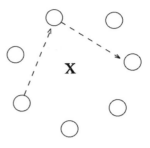

Diagram 3

4) *Pass-to-the-Outside-Hand Drill:* Players work in groups of six. Two groups at one basket, if desired, or groups at a basket.

Offensive players O1, O2 and O3 move the ball around between them by overhead passes. The opposing team (shown as X1, X2 and X3 in diagram 4) is on semi-defense. Player O3 slides and X1 does not front her in this.

All passes must be made to the outside, extended target hand every time. All catches must be performed with the leg on the defender's side, crossing over properly during the catch.

Diagram 4

All six players count passes aloud, and when 25 good ones are achieved, the six players exchange position.

This drill is also a good time to show younger players how passing can be achieved even though both are "covered." The outside hand pass coupled with the crossover leg catch make offenses work!

5) *Passing-on-the-Move-Drill:* This drill is run in 75% of our practices and can be run to either the right or left. Right-handed lay-ups result as show in diagram 5.

Six players begin at passing spots 2, 3, 4, 7, 8 and 9 as shown. They are changed periodically throughout the drill. Player 1 passes to player 2 and begins running straight down the court (at the same time 5 is passing to 7 to start the drill on the other side of the court). Player 2 passes to 1, who then passes to 3. Player 3 returns the pass to 1, who then passes to player 4. Player 4 returns the pass to 1 for a

Diagram 5   Diagram 6

driving lay-up. Player 6 rebounds and passes to 7 to start down the other side. The same action is happening at both ends.

Variations:
- The game clock is set at the two-minute mark and the squad is required to make 25 lay-ups before the horn goes off.
- Sometimes done on only one side, rebound, give ball to permanent passer and then take off for long-pass lay-up.

6) *Diamond 2-on-2 drills:* Lots of emphasis on 2-on-2 play, checking out of shooter and outlet passing. Coach shoots and leaves floor. Teams A and B rebound and pass out to players 1 and 2. They attack at the other end. Teams C and D defend against 1 and 2, rebound and outlet to players 3 and 4. They follow out to the 10-second line to be ready for next turn (see diagram 6).

6) *Ballhandling:* Squad lines up in two lines the length of the floor, about 12 feet apart. Players lined up opposite a partner; one ball to a partnership. Each part of the drill is done eight times and the emphasis of this drill is on quickness.

- *Slams.* Ball is slammed from one hand to another.
- *Fingertip Flips.* Ball is flipped back and forth from hand to hand using the fingertips. Ball can also be moved above the head, eye level, waist level, knee level and back up through various levels.
- *Neck loops.* Around the neck, left to right then right to left.
- *Waist loops.*
- *Knee loops.* Around the right knee, then the left, then both.
- *Figure eight.*
- *Dribbling figure eight.*
- *Two-hand catches.* Ball between legs, body bent, both hands in front holding ball. Ball sent between legs (not touching the floor) and caught with both hands behind legs. Repeat and bring ball and both hands in front. Keep repeating.
- *Alternate catches.* Same as above only start with one hand in front of body and one behind. Keep switching while ball stays constant.
- *Chatter box.* Ball dribbled very low with alternate hands.
- *Tick-tock.* Ball dribbled one bounce through legs, left hand stays in front, right behind.
- *Clap catches.* Ball in front (or behind) at eye level and dropped. Hands clap behind and come back to catch ball.
- *Two-player catch.* Two balls and two players keep them going. Upon catching one, player whips between legs and out with pass to partner.

As more advanced drills are introduced, then the simpler drills at the top of the list are dropped.

Coach Dave Odom
Wake Forest University
Winston-Salem, North Carolina

Stationary Ballhandling Drills

Purpose:

To improve overall ballhandling and passing skills.

Organization:

1) *Body Drill:* Controlling the ball with your fingertips, move the ball in circles as fast as you can.

a) 20 times around the knees

b) 20 time around the waist

c) 20 times around the head

d) Reverse directions and go back up

e) Spread legs: 20 times around each leg

f) Figure eight 20 times

g) Cross-over dribble in front with right hand 20 times, then repeat to the left

2) *Dribbling Circles:* Ball as low to the ground as possible.

a) Right hand only around right leg 20 times

b) Left hand only around left leg 20 times

c) Figure eight/reverse direction, 10 times in each direction

3) *Two Ball Drills*

a) Pound balls the same speed and height for 30 seconds

b) Alternate balls 30 seconds

c) Right high/left low 30 seconds

d) Alternating balls dribble from baseline to baseline -- then repeat using zig zag dribble

4) *Live Ball Moves from Baseline to Baseline:* Make move at each freethrow line and at halfcourt.

a) Stutter step – try to get defender on his heels

b) Cross over

c) Inside-out move – emphasize keeping hand on top of the ball

d) Pull back, cross-over, pull

Scenes from Five-Star

CHAPTER THREE
Passing Drills

Coach Bill Agronin
Niagara University
Niagara University, New York

20-Pass Lay-up Drill

Purpose:
To work on passing, conditioning and concentration (making the lay-up).

Organization:
You will need a minimum of 10 players to complete this drill (12 to 14 works better). Place at least two rebounders at each end and two shooters at the hash marks. Also put a passer on each side of the halfcourt circle. The rebounder takes the ball out of the net and makes a good outlet pass to the shooter who is at the hash mark. The shooter passes to the passer at the halfcourt circle who then returns the ball back to the shooter for a lay-up.

Coaching Points:
- Stress good crisp passes.
- Players must run hard.
- It will take a minute to get 20 or 21 baskets.

Coach Cindy Anderson
Loyola College
Baltimore, Maryland

Four Passes Drill

Purpose: To improve team conditioning, passing and communicating.

Organization:

Time = four minutes   Goal = 82 makes

1) Player 1 outlets to player 2

2) Player 2 turns outside and throws a baseball pass to player 3.

3) Player 3 throws a bounce pass to player 1 who runs the lane line.

4) Player 3 runs outside "coach" and receives a long pass from player 1.

5) Player 1 sprints for a lay-up and sprints to touch the baseline after she passes to player 3.

6) Lines move in direction of pass or "follow your pass."

Coach Cheryl Reeve
Indiana State University
Terre Haute, Indiana

6-Spot Passing Drill

Purpose:

This drill emphasizes passing at a quick pace with accuracy and finishing lay-ups by going up strong to the basket. Points of emphasis in the drill include *passing, communication, finishing* at the basket and *conditioning*.

Organization:

Divide the team in half and put 2:00 on the clock. One half fills the six spots (Group 1) and the other half (Group 2) are passing and finishing lay-ups. Group 1 returns passes that Group 2 makes to them with the final spot on each side of the floor delivering a lead bounce pass that results in the lay-up. Group 2 splits in half with each group beginning the drill on opposite baselines. Players in Group 2 should call the name of the player she is passing to and deliver a crisp chest pass to each spot while running hard in between the spots. At the final spot on that side of the floor, Group 2 players will receive a bounce pass and finish the lay-up. Group 2 should do this for 1:00 and then switch with Group 1. Group 2 would then fill the six spots and Group 1 would pass and finish lay-ups.

You could make this a competitive drill between teams with the team who makes the most lay-ups being the winner OR you could give each team a set number of lay-ups they have to make in a certain time. These are good for keeping the pace of the drill at the desired intensity.

Coach Jill M. Pizzotti
Saint Louis University
St. Louis, Missouri

Circle Passing Drill

Purpose: Teaches players pass fakes and handling pressure.

Organization: Six players line up on the center circle. The remaining players are in a defensive stance along the side. (In the diagram, A and B are defensive players.) The coach gives the ball to a player on the circle. She must complete a pass to another player on the circle, but she cannot throw the ball to a player immediately to her left or right.

Defenses: One defender guards the ball (A), the other reads where the pass is going. The defensive player stays in the circle until she gets a steal or deflection.

Rotation: Bad passer or receiver goes to the end of the defensive stance line. The defender who gets a steal or deflection replaces the bad passer on the circle. The first person in the defensive stance line becomes the defender inside the circle.

Coaching Point: We have the defensive stance line "chop" their feet as the ball is being passed in the circle.

Coach Jessica Smith
Bishop Hartley High School
Columbus, Ohio

Entry Passing

Purpose:
To work on a player's footwork while passing and to become more accurate on the pass.

Organization:
Players will need some masking tape or chalk to make an "X" on the wall or side of their garage at home. The player will take a ball and spin it out (toss it with backspin away from the target). As the player approaches the ball, she will square up and face the target, pivoting first on her right foot. She will make a bounce pass while stepping across the pivot foot (right). The player should continually visualize a defender that she must wrap the pass around. The player will aim for the target each time and check her accuracy. She must keep the ball low to the ground at all times and use her outside hand to make the pass. After mastering this passing technique, the player should practice passing while stepping away from her pivot foot. She must make sure to keep her pivot foot planted so she doesn't travel. Players must be sure to practice using both pivot feet.

Coach Kristy Curry
Purdue University
W. Lafayette, Indiana

Full-Court Passing

Purpose:
Improving passing, shooting, catching, communication and conditioning.

Organization:
Player O1 begins the drill by passing to X1, and runs down the court, O2 does the same with X4. O1 receives pass back from X1 and passes to X2 while continuing down the court. X1, after passing the ball back to O1 goes back to the spot where X2 is. X2 passes back to O1 and goes to the spot where X3 is. O1 receives pass from X2 and passes to X3. X3 receives pass from O1 and passes back to O1, who now shoots a lay-up. X3 follows O1 and rebounds/gets the ball out of net and begins drill down the other side by passing to X8 who has taken X4's spot. O1 goes to the end of line behind X9. Both sides are going concurrently. Right Side: O2 to X4. X4 to O2. O2 to X5. X4 takes X5's spot. X5 to O2. O2 to X6. X5 takes X6's spot. X6 to O2. O2 shoots the lay-up. X6 rebounds and passes to X7.

Coaching Notes:
Kids request this drill daily going full speed passing, catching, communicating, and shooting. This is a great drill. Be sure to set certain goals: no drop passes or push-ups, no missed shots or lay-ups, etc.

Coach Tom Shirley
Philadelphia University
Philadelphia, Pennsylvania

Outlet Drill

Purpose:
Improve overall team performance.

Organization:
Group A: Each player has a ball. In-
dividually, they throw it off the glass
and rebound. They throw an outlet
pass to their partner in Group B.

Group B: Players catch the outlet pass
and dribble once or twice toward the
center circle.

Group C: Players move toward
Group B players to receive pass and
dribble hard once or twice toward
the foul line and pass to shooter in
Group D.

Group D: Each player shoots the ball as directed by the Coach (off dribble,
off catch, lay-up, etc.).

Reverse order to go back down the floor. Players are always moving,
cutting, dribbling, passing and the coaches can step in and defend when-
ever.

Coach Keith Holubesko
Rogers High School
Newport, Rhode Island

Twelve-Second Drill

Purpose:
The twelve-second drill encourages patience and develops the skills needed to pass into the low post successfully

Organization:
Feeding the post is one of the most frequent plays in basketball, but many players do not practice it enough and end up creating a turnover or giving up on the play.

Once a player receives the ball, she has a total of 15 seconds until she has to give it up. Five seconds on the catch, five seconds of dribbling and five more when she picks the ball up. The drill uses 4, 4 and 4 seconds to avoid close calls.

The drills starts with a player spinning out a pass to herself on the wing with a defender playing her. In the low post is an offensive player. After the catch, she must sweep the ball and step (pivot) to create space while looking to pass the ball into the post player. Once four seconds have elapsed, then she must begin to dribble. The player must execute an up two, back two, pullback crossover dribble for four seconds while looking to pass inside. After four seconds, she must pick the ball up. She has four more seconds to sweep and step and pass the ball inside. The type of passes can be a wrap-around bounce, an over-the-head, or a lob. Be sure to fake a pass to make a pass.

This is a great drill that teaches a player to use her time efficiently, as well as working on passing in game situations. The results are less forced turnovers and more successful low post entries.

Coach Greg T. Collins
DuPont Manual High School
Louisville, Kentucky

Bad Pass/Good Catch Drill

Diagram 1   *Diagram 2*

Purpose:

To improve a player's ability to catch all passes.

Organization:

One offensive post player, two passers on opposite sides of the court each with a basketball.

1) Player 1 throws a bad pass (too high, too low, etc.) and then calls the post player's name as soon as the pass is released (see diagram 1).

2) Upon hearing her name called, the post player turns and comes toward the bad pass, catches the pass and scores.

3) The shooter gets the ball out of the net and quickly passes back to the player who passed it. The post player simultaneously gets out of the lane (see diagram 2).

4) As soon as the post player's feet hit the floor outside the lane, the player on the opposite side throws a bad pass and calls the post player's name to continue the drill.

Coaching Points:
- ♦ Passers challenge the post player.

Coach Bob Starkman
Broward Community College
Ft. Lauderdale, Florida

Weak Hand Pass and Catch

Purpose:
To develop overall team catching and shooting, weak hand passing and catching – quick jump shooting, one player at a time.

Organization:
The coach passes the ball to player. Player returns the pass with her weak hand. The coach passes back right away; player catches and shoots. Player then quickly moves to another spot on the floor (circles perimeter) and continues the drill. Positions for shooting include wing, wing, top of key, wing, wing – then go back the opposite way.

Scenes from Five-Star

CHAPTER FOUR
Shooting and Offensive Concepts

Coach Amy Meehan
Drury High School
North Adams, Massachusetts

Points in Shooting

Purpose: Listed below are points of concern which should be kept in mind when working on a player's shooting skills.

The Jump Shot:

1) *Stance and Body Balance*
   a. Keep feet squared to the basket, with the right foot pointed at the basket.
   b. Feet should be about shoulder-width apart, with the toes in line or the shooting-arm foot in a toe-instep relation with the other foot (right foot forward for right-handers).
   c. Body Balance — weight on the balls of the feet and heels in contact with the floor.
   d. Low going into the jump shot.
   e. Head up and hips in line with the feet.
   f. Keep shoulders squared to the basket and back relatively straight.
   g. Head should be up with good court vision while keeping the head above and between the feet and still.
   h. Always catch the ball in triple threat position (shoot, pass dribble). Prepare quickly to shoot as opposed to shooting quickly.

2) *Hand Placement*
   a. Ball should be gripped only by the pads of the fingers (first and second joints).
   b. Both the guide hand and shooting hand should be slightly cupped, being relaxed, not tense!

c. Shooting hand behind the ball and guide hand on the side. Not under and in front of the ball.

   d. The ball should be kept close to the body for protection and in a position to react.

   e. The shooting hand should be rotated or positioned behind the ball as soon as possible. The index finger should be on the valve stem and pointed straight ahead. The index finger and the thumb should form a "J."

   f. The wrist should be cocked (look for wrinkles) as soon as the ball is pulled into the body to the triple threat position.

3) *Position of the Elbow*

   a. Position should be natural, relaxed and under the ball. Not pointed outward!

   b. Elbow should be in front of the ball and toward the midline of the body.

   c. Work to keep the right foot, knee, hip, elbow and ball all in one line.

4) *Sighting the Basket*

   a. Pick an imaginary spot (black dot) somewhere inside the rim where you want the ball to drop through the hoop.

   b. Do not watch the ball!

   c. When using the backboard, keep your eyes on the spot and the ball should hit the spot as it descends.

   d. Use the backboard on 45-degree angle shots up to 10 feet, and always on lay-ups.

   e. Keep the head still and not tilted back.

5) *Lift and Release*

   a. As the ball is brought into the shooting position, the elbow is in and the wrist is cocked.

   b. The elbow should be ahead of the ball and pointed toward the basket area.

   c. A "C" is developed between the back of the hand, forearm and the upper arm of the shooting arm.

   d. The elbow should act as a hinge.

   e. As the ball is started forward toward the basket, the elbow unlocks (extension of the arm), then the wrist is uncocked, snapped completely forward completing the follow-through.

f. The arm should be completely extended toward the middle of the basket with the wrist snapped vertically, pointing the middle finger toward the basket. Hold this follow-through position as long as possible.

g. The wrist, elbow and arm merely accentuate the momentum started in the legs.

h. The elevation of the jump shot should be straight up with no flotation right, left, front or back. You should land in the same spot you took off in or slightly closer to the basket, (6" at most) and never should you land going backward).

i. Extend the ankles on the jump shot for better body control, alignment, lift and cushioned landing from which to react quickly.

j. Release the ball just before or at the peak of your jump.

6) *Flight of the Ball*
   a. The arm should be extended up and through the basket, not at it!
   b. Do not watch the ball, keep rim vision.
   c. The vertical wrist snap should provide the necessary backspin.
   d. Exaggerate the arm extension and hold it for a better trajectory.
   e. Ball should be shot at a 60-degree arch.

7) *Concentration*
   a. A shooter must concentrate on the basket or she will miss the easiest of shots.
   b. Concentrate on the fundamentals of good shooting and beware of corrections to be made.
   c. Concentrate on the basket regardless of defensive hands, talking or any other defensive distractions.
   d. Concentrate on taking high-percentage shots.

8) *Most Common Mistakes*
   a. Index finger not on center.
   b. Footwork and stance not in balance.
   c. Lifting ball too soon or improper release.
   d. Twisting the lift hand or "J" thumb through shot.
   e. Improper follow-through.
   f. Watching the ball after release.
   g. Not locking out shooting arm, and holding it.

> h. Shot selection. Know your shooting range.

9) *Missed Shots*
   a. Shots off to the side: check alignment, hands, follow-through, takeoff/landing point.
   b. Short shots: check shooting pocket height, may need more knee bend, may be releasing ball on the way down, may need more arch, may be out of your range.
   c. Shots long: may need less knee bend, may be releasing ball too early, may need less arch.
   d. Shots heavy: check rotation (wrist snap), may need more arch.

Good shooters make corrections during the game. Be confident in your ability to shoot the basketball. Good shooters are not born, they are made. Do your work and it will pay off!

Coach Brenda Oldfield
Ball State University
Muncie, Indiana

1:30 Free-Throw Drill

Diagram 1

Diagram 2

Purpose:
To improve free-throw shooting.

Organization:
Pairup players and set the clock to 1 minute and 30 seconds. The first partner gets up and begins shooting her freethrows. She must make three in a **row** to complete her part of the drill. Her partner rebounds the ball back to her. (See Diagram 1)

Once the first partner finishes making three shots in a row, then the second partner gets up and shoots. She must make three freethrows in a row as well. However, depending on how little or much time was used by the first shooter will determine how much time the last shooter has. The two combined only get 1:30. If they don't complete the drill on time, we repeat the drill until they finish. This drill can also be done in a team setting, with one pair competing against another. (See Diagram 2)

Coach Sylvia Hatchell
University of North Carolina
Chapel Hill, North Carolina

3-Player/2-Ball Shooting Drill

Purpose:
To improve shooting and rebounding under game conditions.

Organization:
Player 1 will shoot the ball, then go and get her own rebound and make a hard game-style pass to player 3. After player 1 shoots, player 2 will shoot the second ball and go get her own rebound and make a pass to player 1. Player 3 will shoot, then go get her own rebound and make a pass to player 2. These three players will do the continuous shooting drill at a fast pace, taking game shots for a set period of time (usually one minute). Three new players step in and keep the drill going when the minute is up — rotation is shoot 3 minutes, rest 3 minutes.

Coach Cindy Anderson
Loyola College
Baltimore, Maryland

30-Point Shooting Drill

Purpose: To develop three-dimensional shooting skills.

Organization:
1) As per the diagram, mark out five distinct spots for shooter to stand.

2) Each shooter will take three shots from a spot:

♦ First shot is a "3" — The player earns 3 points if it is made
♦ Second shot is a shot fake and dribble for pull-up hard — The player earns 2 points if it is made
♦ Third shot is a shot fake and hard dribble to basket for a lay-up — The player earns 1 point if made to the basket

3) After the third shot from spot X1, the player moves to spot X2 and so on.

Partner rebounds and keeps score.

Coach Debbie Taneyhill
George Mason University
Fairfax, Virginia

Four-Minute Shooting Drill

Purpose:

This is a competitive drill we often use at the end of practice or right before a break. The team will shoot from each spot on the floor (both corners and both elbows) for one minute each. A coach is in charge of keeping score. A field goal is one point, a three-point shot is worth two points.

Organization:

Begin the drill with half the team in the corner and the other half at the elbow. The first two people at the elbow need a ball. The ball is passed from the elbow to the corner — shooter gets her own rebound and passer follows the pass and goes to the end of the line. After the shooter gets her rebound, she passes out to the elbow and goes to the end of the line.

After the first minute, both lines shift — the corner line goes to elbow, elbow goes to other elbow, balls stay in the same line. Shots now go up from the elbow.

Switch again after second minute — elbow to corner, elbow to elbow. Shots continue to go up from elbow.

To start the fourth minute, lines stay in the same spots, but pass comes from the elbow to the corner for shot. For the last spot, players have the option of calling "post" and running to block to receive the pass for a lay-up. (See the diagram, pass must go from elbow to corner to post.) Team must communicate.

Make the drill competitive by giving each team a target total of points. We try to get 80 or higher in four minutes. Total number of points can be adjusted to skill level and familiarity with the drill.

Coach Brenda Oldfield
Ball State University
Muncie, Indiana

Ball State Shooting Drills

Purpose: To improve overall shooting ability.

5-Spot 3-Point Shooting Drill
Organization: The object of the drill is to make a total of five three-point baskets from each spot. After making five from one spot, a player moves to the next spot. Drill can be timed to make it more competitive. Players can compete against each other or aim for a time under 2.5 minutes. (See Diagram 1)

Diagram 1

3 Players/2 Balls
Organization: We then put three players on the floor with two balls to use between them. The first player steps up to the first spot as the shooter. We then set up one passer and one rebounder. The passer constantly feeds the shooter with balls, the rebounder rebounds and feeds the passer with balls. They do this until the shooter makes five shots from that spot. (See Diagram 2) After making five shots, the shooter moves to the next spot. The passer and rebounder move accordingly. They repeat the same action until the shooter makes five shots again. They continue this through all five spots. Once the drill is finished, the shooter will have made 25 three-point shots. (See Diagram 3)

Diagram 2

Diagram 3

Coach Kevin Chaney
Solono Community College
Suisun City, California

Three-Point/Chair Shooting

"3 PT SHOOTING" (4)

Diagram 1

"CHAIR SHOOTING" (2)

Diagram 2

Purpose:
To develop three-point shooting ability.

Organization:
At one basket, the shooter goes around twice shooting 11 three-pointers. The shooter is to focus on good and proper footwork and quick release. (See Diagram 1)

Goal:
Footwork for three-pointers. Quick Release and hustling to each chair to simulate coming off screens to shoot.

At a second basket, place a chair just in front of the rim, start shot at 90 degrees and snap wrist up and out while shooting up and over the rim. (See Diagram 2)

Goal: Develop shot release, wrist snap and shot arch. Perfect for injured players too!

Rotation: S goes to CR position, R2 goes to R1, R goes to S, CS becomes R2, R1 becomes R, and CR becomes CS.

Coach Kevin Chaney
Solono Community College
Suisun City, California

"Circuit" Jump Shot Routine

Purpose:

To develop the jump shot. To break down the proper footwork to beat the defense and take a good percentage shot. Start at the #1 spot in diagram. Do the two-minute circuit, then move to spot #2 and repeat. It's a 10-minute drill, utilizing five spots on the court. The drill should always be done at game speed.

Organization:

Start by putting 10 minutes on the game clock. Assign two players per basket — more players may be added if necessary. Every player has a ball. Have players start at the top of the key. Blow whistle to indicate time to change position. The first 30 seconds are occupied by the players shooting the right, left, right jump shot. The next 30, flip pass right, left, right jump shot. Thirty seconds then are spent on the pump fake, step hop jump shot, and then reverse it for the next 30 seconds, pump fake crossover, step hop jump shot. Go to the right wing and repeat until all five spots are done.

Coach Jack Miller
Rider University
Lawrenceville, New Jersey

Competitive Shooting Drill

Purpose: To improve shooting skills

Organization: Players start in a line at the left corner of the baseline. Set a chair on the three-point arc in the left and right corner of the baseline.

1) Player 1 starts by making a one-on-one move around the chair. The progression of shots is as follows:
   a) Pump fake, swing the ball to the right, take one dribble to the middle for a shot.
   b) Pump fake, swing the ball to the left, take one dribble to the baseline for a shot.
   c) Pump fake, swing the ball to the right, take one dribble to the middle, then use a crossover dribble behind the chair, take another dribble to the baseline for a shot.
   d) Pump fake, swing the ball to the left, take one dribble to the baseline, then use a crossover dribble behind the chair, take another dribble to the middle for a shot.

2) Players 2, 3 and 4 follow player 1. After each shot, the players go to the right corner and use the same shots. The progression on the right side is as follows:

a) Pump fake, swing the ball to the right, and take one dribble to the baseline for a shot.

b) Pump fake, swing the ball to the left, take one dribble to the middle for a shot.

c) Pump fake, swing the ball to the right, take one dribble to the baseline, then use a crossover dribble behind the chair, take another dribble to the middle for a shot.

d) Pump fake, swing the ball to the left, take one dribble to the middle, then use a crossover dribble behind the chair, take another dribble to the baseline for a shot.

3) First player to make 10 shots is the winner.

Coach Bill Agronin
Niagara University
Niagara University, New York

Continuous Lay-up Drill

Purpose:

To improve game conditioning and shooting.

Organization:

1) A1 dribbles and makes basket, goes to end of B line. A2 follows up A1's shot and outlets to B1. (See Diagram 1)

Diagram 1

2) B1 passes to C1. C1 passes to A2, who sprints to the three-point line. C1 goes to the top line behind A3. A2 passes to B1. (See Diagram 2)

Diagram 2

3) B1 passes back to A2 for shot (lay-up). B1 goes to end of C line. (See Diagram 3)

4) A2 makes lay-up, goes to end of B line. A3 shoots follow-up lay-up and outlets to B2. B2 passes to C2. A2 sprints to the three-point line. (See Diagram 4)

Diagram 3

5) C2 passes back to A3 then C2 goes to the top line behind C1. (See Diagram 5)

Diagram 4

Diagram 5

Diagram 6

6) A3 passes to B2, and A3 sprints to receive pass from B2. Drill continues until goal of made lay-ups is reached. (See Diagrams 6 and 7)

Diagram 7

Coach Tom Weaver
Albany College of Pharmacy
Albany, New York

Foul-Shot Golf

Purpose:
This drill is a fun way to practice shooting free throws.

Organization:
The players play 18 "holes" by rotating to different baskets in our gym. Each basket is a par-2 with a maximum of five attempts. Score is kept on cards obtained from a miniature golf course. The winner gets to sit out line drills, slides or foot fires at the next practice.

Coaching Notes:
- Replace all divots.
- Do not attempt to play out of sand traps.
- Our best free-throw shooter has been consistently scoring -9.

Hole	Par				
1	2				
2	2				
3	2				
4	2				
5	2				
6	2				
7	2				
8	2				
9	2				
10	2				
11	2				
12	2				
13	2				
14	2				
15	2				
16	2				
17	2				
18	2				
Total	36				

Coach Bob Foley
University of Richmond
Richmond, Virginia

Sprint Shooting

Purpose:

To shoot at game speed, game condition and game specificiations.

Organization:

All six passers (P) have basketballs. On the whistle, the Ss run their fast-break lanes. The three P's pass to the player on their wing (or middle). The S's shoot, get their own rebound and fill the three P spots. The P's

Diagram 1

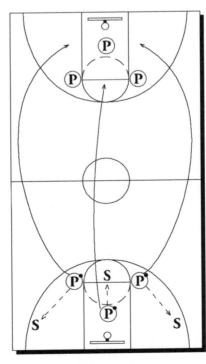

Diagram 2

spring to their respective fast-break positions downcourt for a pass and shot.

We run this drill continuously for two minutes. We get great conditioning, shoot approximately 75 shots off transition, and the players enjoy it. We set a goal of 55 to 60 made shots and take a water break if successful.

Coaching Points:
- ◆ Run your lanes wide, full spring into a control run, then into footwork for a balanced shot.
- ◆ We also make it mandatory that our wings shoot bank shots.

Coach Cheryl Dozier
University at Buffalo
Buffalo, New York

Star Shooting

Our philosophy at the University at Buffalo, like all team philosophies, has several different aspects to it. One of our beliefs, however, is that no matter what, we will be in the best possible condition that we can be. We try to incorporate conditioning into all of our drills, and the following drill is just an example of how we do this.

Diagram 1

Purpose:
To teach players to shoot properly when tired.

Organization:
This drill can be done with one or two players.

1) Player 1 shoots first, while player 2 rebounds and passes. Player 1 starts on the baseline and simply sprints from spot to spot catching and shooting.
2) After player 1 finishes her last shot (taken from the elbow), she follows her shot, puts it back if it is a miss, and then passes it out to player 2 for her shots.

Coaching Points:
- We emphasize the technical aspects of shooting: footwork, follow-through, body-balance, etc.
- It is also important that the player *sprints* from spot to spot to emphasize shooting while tired.

Coach Bill Agronin
Niagara University
Niagara University, New York

Three-Down Shooting

Diagram 1: *To start the "three down shooting" drill, put three players on each baseline and three at half court.*

Purpose:
To improve three-point shooting. This drill can be used anytime during practice, but we have found it is most effective at the end as our last drill.

Organization:
You need a minimum of nine players to run the drill. There is no maximum, but, 12 is ideal. We begin with three players on each baseline and three players at half-court. Each player on the baseline has a ball. As the players from half-court run toward the baseline, a ball is passed to each player. After passing the ball, the passer runs toward the opposite basket. The players shoot when they receive the pass. A three-point shot counts three, inside the arc a jumper counts two, and anything in the "paint" counts one point. The drill goes for one minute. If the team scores a predetermined number of points, the drill is over. If the score is not achieved, they do it again. We start the season with a goal of 60 points. As the season progresses we move our goal up to 65, then 70 points. Each shooter must get her rebound and be ready to pass to the next player coming down into her zone.

Coaching Points:

♦ A coach or manager should be stationed at each baseline to count the points.

♦ The players like the drill because it is competitive and there is a goal to meet.

♦ Coaches like it because it is a good conditioning, shooting and passing drill. You should emphasize squaring up before taking a shot and also making a good pass to the shooter. Limit the three-point shots to your better shooters. All others should shoot inside the arc.

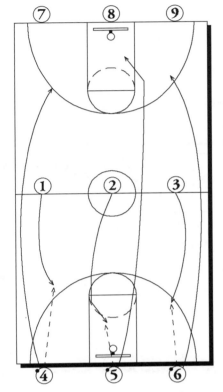

Diagram 2: The passers move down the court to the opposite baseline ready to receive a pass and shot.

Coach Sylvia Hatchell
University of North Carolina
Chapel Hill, North Carolina

Triangle Shooting Drill

Purpose:
To improve perimeter shooting.

Organization:
Shooting area is three places on the court: right side, top and left side. Shooter will move within a 12-foot area. You have a shooter, a rebounder and a passer. Rotate every 30 seconds (or 45 seconds or 60 seconds, depending on how long you have to conduct the drill). Use two balls. The shooter will shoot as many shots as possible in the time period allowed. Players will rotate from passer to shooter, shooter to rebounder, and rebounder to passer.

Coach Charlene Curtis
Wake Forest University
Winston-Salem, North Carolina

1-on-1 Offensive Moves

Purpose: To develop a player's total offensive game and not limit them to one move. Basic 1-on-1 offensive moves when facing the basket can be used from any position on the floor.

Coaching Tips:
1) *Getting Open.* Use a change of pace with a change of direction to get open to receive the ball.
    a) V-cut. Turn your body toward the basket. Take two or three steps, plant your inside foot (the foot closest to the baseline), and push off toward the ball to receive the pass. Your movement is in the shape of a "V."
    b) L-cut. Start away from the ball. Take two or three steps straight toward the ball. Plant your inside foot and push off at a 45-degree angle to receive the pass. Your movement is in the shape of an "L."

2) *Receiving the Pass.* Call for the ball when you are ready to receive it. Extend your arms with your palms facing the ball. Your fingers should be relaxed and your elbows slightly bent.

3) *Facing the Basket.* Turning to face the basket allows you to see the basket, your defender and your teammates.
    a) Pivoting. Using your inside foot (the foot closest to the basket), lift your heel slightly off the floor, then turn and face the basket.
    b) Triple-threat position. Position the ball in front of you so you can shoot it, pass it or dribble it. You may bring the ball to this posi-

tion by swinging it quickly by your knees, across your chest, or up and across your forehead.

4) *Attacking the Defender*. All 1-on-1 moves begin with a short jab step made with the nonpivot foot (the foot farthest from the basket when you pivoted). The jab step may be a part of the pivot or an additional step after you pivot. The best offenseive moves are made toward the defender's front foot. To simplify the explanation of these moves, the defender's front foot is on the same side as the jab step in all of these situations. Your left foot is your pivot foot and your right foot is your jab foot. (The same move can be made with your right foot as your pivot foot and your left foot as your jab foot.)

a) *Jab step*. With your knees bent and maintaining a triple-threat position, move your right foot forward while leaning slightly over the foot. This movement gives the defender the impression that you are moving in that direction. The jab step should be short enough for you to remain balanced.

It is important that you first work hard to get open; second, ask for the ball by calling for it and extending your arms, and then square up and face the basket. Attacking the defender's front foot makes the most effective 1-on-1 move. Take your time and read the defender's stance, then attack the front foot.

Coach Jessica Smith
Bishop Hartley High School
Columbus, Ohio

Jab Series: Footwork

Purpose:

To master the footwork from a triple-threat position.

Organization:

The player begins on the left side of the basket about 15 feet out on the baseline. Before each move, the player will spin the ball out (toss it with backspin toward the free-throw line). As the player approaches the ball, she will square up to the basket on her inside foot (in this case, her left) as she catches the ball. She will bend her knees and sit down so she is quick in her motions. At this point, follow the individual moves for the players to work on:

1) *Jab and Go*: While squared up, the player will jab with her right foot (take a small hard step forward with only one foot, so she doesn't travel) and keep the ball on the right side of her body. Then the player will accelerate in that same direction by restepping with that same foot and taking a dribble on the outside of the right foot. At this point, she explodes to the rim for a lay-up using one or two dribbles.

2) *Jab and Crossover*: While squared up, the player will jab with her right foot, with the ball on her right side, then swing the ball through to the left side with a quick sweeping motion at knee level and cross her right foot over her left (without moving the left). Finally, she will explode to the basket using one or two dribbles.

3) *Square and Shoot*: Once squared up, the player will go right into her shot.

4) *Jab and Shoot*: Once squared up, the player will jab with her right foot and bring it back to square position; staying low, she will then shoot.

After finishing all these moves from the left side of the basket, the player will move to the opposite side of the basket and repeat the jab series from the right side.

Coach Duffy Burns
Cleveland State University
Cleveland, Ohio

Perimeter Moves

Diagram 1

Diagram 2

Diagram 3

Purpose:
To enhance the development of perimeter players.

Organization:

1) Left Foot is always the pivot foot. Direct Cross. (See Diagram 1)

Diagram 4

2) Fake Cross (See Diagram 2)

3) Back Off (See Diagram 3)

4) Fake Back Off (See Diagram 4)

Coach Joe McKeown
George Washington University
Washington, D.C.

Snap, Crackle, Pop

Diagram 1

Diagram 2

Purpose:
To develop screening/base of the screen.

Organization:
1) Player X1 passes to the coach and screens for player X2.

2) Player X2 curls to the basket and X1 pops back for the shot.

3) Add defensive players and rotate.

Coach Bob Foley
University of Richmond
Richmond, Virginia

Two Ball Screen Drill

Purpose:
Setting and using screens to improve footwork.

Diagram 1

Diagram 2

Organization:
Players start in four lines.
P= Passing Lines
S= Shooting Lines
S1 Sets a screen on M (Managers) for S-2

S2 can (4 options):
1) Flash to the ball
2) Fade off the screen
3) Curl to the basket
4) Cut backdoor off the screen

Diagram 4

Diagram 3

S1 reads where S2 cuts and rolls to the appropriate spot. P1 passes to the cutter going to the basket, P2 passes to the cutter going to the high post area for a jumper. S1 and S2 get their own rebounds and get into the passing line. P1 and P2 go to the shooting lines.

The drill focuses on how to read screens and how the screener reacts to that read. We also stress the footwork on the approach and the explosion off the screens, as well as the screener coming back to the ball and looking for her own shot.

Coach Duffy Burns
Cleveland State University
Cleveland, Ohio

12 Ways to 3

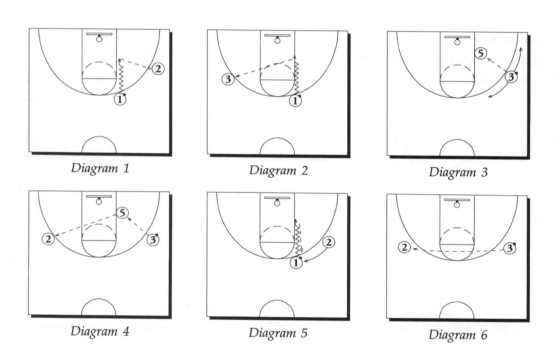

Diagram 1   Diagram 2   Diagram 3

Diagram 4   Diagram 5   Diagram 6

Purpose: To break down every possible 3-point opportunity that a team might get in transition or on offense.

Organization:

1) Penetrate and pitch — same side (See Diagram 1)

2) Penetrate and pitch — opposite side (See Diagram 2)

3) Inside-out — same side (See Diagram 3)

Diagram 7

Diagram 8

Diagram 9

Diagram 10

Diagram 11

Diagram 12

4) Inside-out — opposite side (See Diagram 4)

5) Fill the hole (See Diagram 5)

6) Skip pass (See Diagram 6)

7) Screen-and-roll (See Diagram 7)

8) Screen-and-pop (See Diagram 8)

9) Screen-and-pop — top of key (See Diagram 9)

10) Deep curl (See Diagram 10)

11) Staggered double (See Diagram 11)

12) Back-screen lob(See Diagram 12)

Coach Duffy Burns
Cleveland State University
Cleveland, Ohio

30-Second Drills

Diagram 1   Diagram 2   Diagram 3)

Diagram 4   Diagram 5

Purpose:
To break down different aspects of offense and rebounding and enhance the "team" concept. Repetition creates good habits.

Organization:
1) Pivot and protect (See Diagram 1)
2) Passing and cutting (See Diagram 2)
3) Pass and relocate (See Diagram 3)
4) Run at the shooter: (See Diagram 4)
   Paired shooting — 5 spots

112

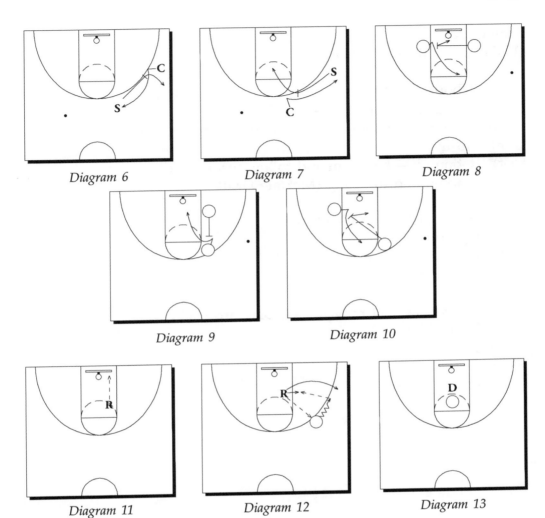

Diagram 6   Diagram 7   Diagram 8

Diagram 9   Diagram 10

Diagram 11   Diagram 12   Diagram 13

    a) Shoulders in front of feet
    b) Hands ready
    c) Catch shoot
    d) Make 5 rotate to next spot
Paired shooting with shot fake and one dribble (See Diagram 5)
    a) Shot fake — shooting pocket to forehead
    b) One dribble — go thru defense
5) Buddy screening (perimeter) Down screen (See Diagram 6)
6) Back screen (See Diagram 7)
7) Buddy screening (inside) cross screen (See Diagram 8)
8) Back screen (See Diagram 9)
9) Down screen (See Diagram 10)

Timing Drills
1) Throw off Board (See Diagram 11)
   a) Rebound
   b) Rebound and follow
   c) Rebound — shot fake and follow
   d) Rebound — shot fake and follow reverse lay-up
   e) Tip-in
   f) Rebound — back rim and follow (backboard)
   g) Tipping and touching (McHale Drill)

2) Rebound and Outlet (See Diagram 12)
   a) Rebound — outlet
   b) Post up — move
   c) Bang the board (3 times)

3) Post moves (1-on-1 moves) (See Diagram 13)
   a) No dribble
   b) 1 dribble

4) Perimeter moves
   a) 1 dribble
   b) 2 dribble

Coach Belinda "Boe" Pearman
University of Rhode Island
Kingston, Rhode Island

Zone Coverage Breakdown

Diagram 1

Diagram 2

Diagram 3

Purpose:
Work on zone coverage in breakdown situations.

Organization:

Guard Coverage
Set up the drill with two guards on defense and four offensive players outside the three-point line.
1) Player starts with ball and defenders must guard ball and defend the next pass.
2) Offensive players remain stationary and pass the ball only on coach's command.

Post Coverage
1) Coach passes ball to the corner offensive player and wing defender must cover, while post defender goes "top side" to baseline coverage.
2) On pass to high post, post defender goes "top side" and wing defender comes back to coverage.

Coach Craig Kennedy
Auburn University
Auburn, Alabama

Initiating a Drive

Diagram 1

Diagram 2

Purpose:
This drill teaches players to learn how to read the defender and drive for a lay-up or jump shot.

Organization:
Set goals of so many made hoops in a row, or a total number of shots. You need a minimum of three people and one basketball. The rotation is always as follows: follow your pass and play cooperative or live defense, replace the person you guard, score, rebound, pass, play defense and replace.

Have players in three lines under the basket with the ball in the middle line (diagram 1). Player 1 has the ball and passes out to 2. Player 1 goes and plays defense on 2. At first have the defenders play cooperative defense and take away a designated side, either baseline or middle. Drills can become operational or live after players learn to read and respond. The defender now replaces 2 on the wing (see diagram 2). Player 2 drives around the defender for a lay-up (see diagram 3). Player 2 finishes her shot if she misses, and then goes

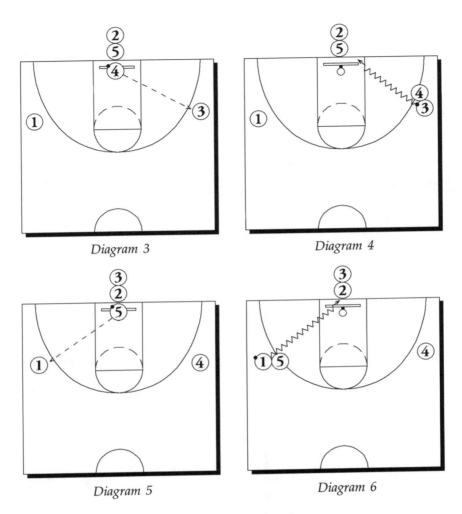

Diagram 3

Diagram 4

Diagram 5

Diagram 6

to the back of the line. Player 4 passes out to 3, and plays defense (see diagram 4). Player 3 drives at the defender for a lay-up (see diagram 4). Player 3 finishes her shot if missed. Player 5 passes the ball and goes and plays defense on 1 (see diagram 6).

This drill can be the same as "screen to three jumpers" and use only three players at each hoop. Players can learn to use shot fakes to bring the defender out to create space for the drive. Have players finish off if they miss, and always catch the rebound in the air. Encourage the last person to drive in for a lay-up or a close jumper if the first two have missed, so that players understand the need to take a high-percentage shot and stop their own scoring slumps. This drill also moves nicely into a 2-on-1 full-court drill or a 2-on-1 half-court drill if the coach wants.

Coach Craig Kennedy
Auburn University
Auburn, Alabama

Read and Lead

Diagram 1   Diagram 2

Purpose:

This drill teaches players to read the defender on a transition situation.

Organization:

Have one group of players on the end line to rebound and one group on the sideline at the outlet position. Have another group at the other end, but on the same side of the floor at the time line. Have a defender

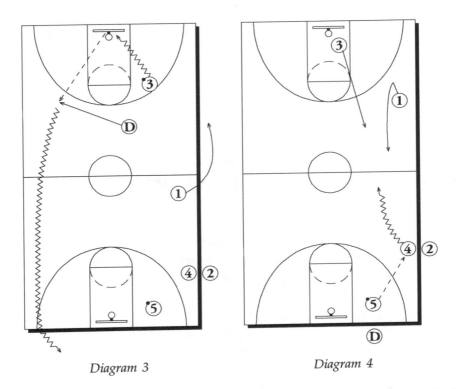

Diagram 3   *Diagram 4*

downcourt who can either look to deny the lead pass or protect the basket (see diagram 1). Player 2 tosses the ball off of the backboard to simulate a rebound and then makes an outlet pass to player 1. Player 2 passes
and goes to the back of the outlet line (see diagram 1).

Player 1 takes the ball on the dribble and reads when her teammate 3 is
open. Player 1 has to pass before she crosses the center line (see diagram
2). When player 3 gets the ball, she goes one-on-one with D. After scoring, player 3 makes an outlet pass to the defender "D" who goes the
length of the floor for a lay-up or jump shot and joins the rebound line.

The person who played offense during one-on-one (3) now becomes
the defender, the person who made the lead pass (1) now becomes the
offensive player for one-on-one. The next player in the outlet line steps
onto the court. The rebounder tosses the ball up off of the backboard and
the drill continues (see diagram 4).

This is another drill that can become a 2-on-1 on the way back if the
coach desires. Have the defenders vary whether they will deny or protect so that the ball handler learns to "read and respond" and make the
appropriate pass.

Coach Craig Kennedy
Auburn University
Auburn, Alabama

Screen to Three Lay-ups

Diagram 1

Purpose:
This is a drill that combines passing, setting, and using screens for both a shot or a drive.

Organization:
Set goals of so many made hoops in a row or a total number or shots. You need a minimum of three people and one basketball. The rotation is always as follows: follow your pass and set a ball screen, replace the person you screen, score, rebound, pass, ball screen and replace.

Have players in three lines at center with the ball in the middle line (see diagram 1). Player 1 has the ball and passes ahead to 2. Player 1 sets a ball screen for 2 and replaces 2 on the wing (see diagram 2). Player 2 drives around the screen for a lay-up (see diagram 3). Player 2 finishes her shot if she misses, and rebounds her own shot. Player 2 passes out to 3 and sets a ball screen (see diagram 4). Player 3 drives off of the screen for a lay-up (see diagram 5). Player 3 rebounds her own

Diagram 2

shot and passes and ball screens for 1 (see diagram 6). Player 1 drives for a lay-up and rebounds her own shot (see diagram 7). To complete the drill, player 1 makes an outlet pass and the outlet relays the ball to the

120

middle person of the next group (see diagram 8). 1-2-3 go off the side of the court so that next group can go.

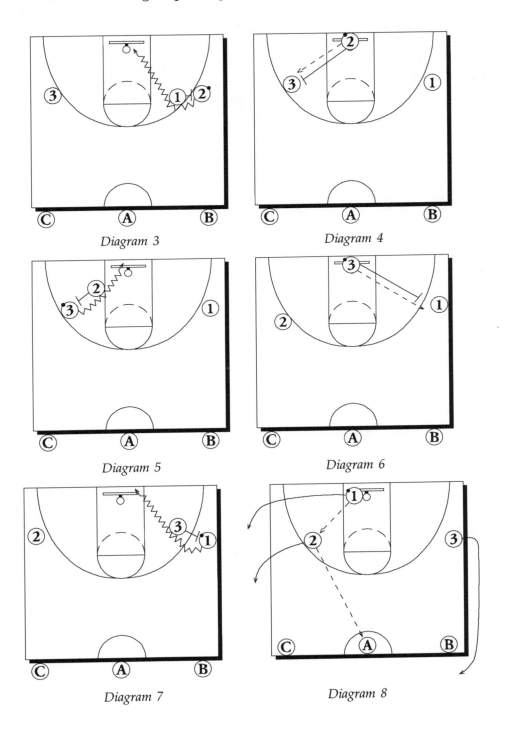

Diagram 3

Diagram 4

Diagram 5

Diagram 6

Diagram 7

Diagram 8

This drill can be done using jump shots around or over the screen. I like to have players call the name of the person they are screening for and use a hand signal to indicate what side of the screen to use. Have players finish off if they miss and always catch the rebound in the air. When shooting jump shots, I have consequences when all three do not score. Encourage the last person to drive in for a lay-up or a close jumper if the first two have missed so that players understand the need to take high percentage shots and stop their own scoring slumps. This drill moves nicely into a 2-on-1 full-court drill or a 2-on-1 half-court drill if the coach wants.

Coach Craig Kennedy
Auburn University
Auburn, Alabama

Four Corners to a Lay-up

Purpose:
To improve ballhandling, outlet and lead passes, and basic give-and-go play and lay-ups.

Organization:
You need two basketballs and a minimum of six players. Place your team in four groups, one at each foul-line extended (see diagram 1). The groups will always go diagonally. The rotation is as follows:

Diagram 1

1. Outlet pass to the side outlet pass, follow the pass and go to the back of the line.

2. Catch the outlet pass, make a fast-break pass or go on a transition dribble and make a lead pass.

3. Make a basket cut and lay-up (give and go).

4. After the lay-up, make an outlet pass. Follow the pass and go to the back of the line. Always outlet to the same person who gave the give-and-go pass.

123

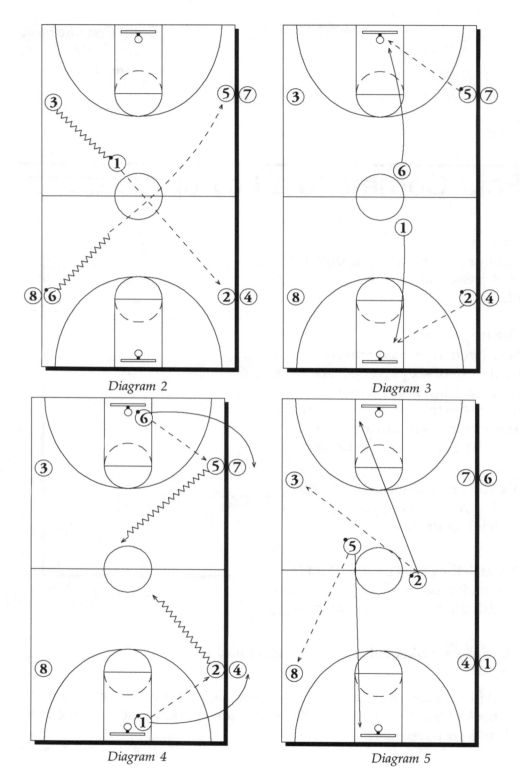

Diagram 2

Diagram 3

Diagram 4

Diagram 5

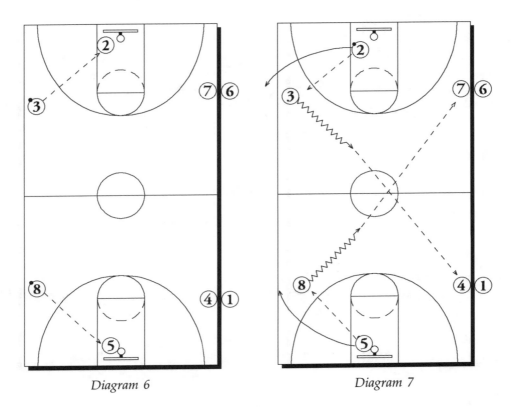

Diagram 6   Diagram 7

Start with one ball at each end of the court. Player 1 starts with the ball and advances the ball diagonally up the court either by a fastbreak pass or by taking it on the dribble then leading it ahead (see diagram 2). After passing the ball, player 1 cuts to the basket for a give and go pass. Have the passers work on faking a pass first, then hitting the cutter on the block for the lay-up (see diagram 3). After scoring the lay-up, player 1 takes the rebound, pivots and makes an outlet pass to player 2. Player 1 now goes to the back of the line (see diagram 4). Player 2 takes the ball diagonally and leads it ahead to player 3 and then 2 cuts to the basket on the give-and-go (see diagrams 5-7). Remember that the lines are always going diagonally.

While this is going on, the other group is following the same procedure in the other direction. Groups will either be doing left- or right-handed lay-ups. Always demand that they execute right-hand lay-ups on the right side and left-hand lay-ups on the left side. After reaching your goal (10 in total or eight in a row), the teams switch sides of the court to work on lay-ups with their other hand (see diagram 8).

Diagram 8

Diagram 9

Diagram 10

Variations include power lay-ups, reverse lay-ups, catch at the high post and execute a shot or pass fake and then drive (see diagram 9), fake and cross-over (see diagram 10), etc. If one end reaches their goal first, I have them work on jump shots until both ends reach their target. To increase the difficulty of this drill, have players execute a behind-the-back dribble or between-the-legs dribble, or some other dribble variation at center before they make the lead pass.

CHAPTER FIVE

Transition Game: Offense and Defense

Coach Stephen Post
Manhattanville College
Purchase, New York

Fast-Break Drills: Offense and Defense

Purpose:

These are a series of four drills that we use as a conditioner and warm-up usually at the beginning of practice. The drills incorporate 2-on-1 and 3-on-2 fast-break offense and defense as well as 1-on-2 and 2-on-3 press offense and defense. Each drill is done for three minutes.

Organization:

Three-Drill Offense

The players line up along the baseline as shown in diagram A with players 1, 4 and 7 with a ball. Player 1 dribbles the length of the floor to make a lay-up at the other end. Player 2 retrieves the ball and takes it out-of-bounds. If player 1 misses the lay-up, the coach has player 2 take the ball out-of-bounds or just rebound the ball and continue the ball from there. Player 3 is going to defend player 1 and try to deny the ball inbounds from player 2. The inbounds pass cannot go past the foul-line extended. Players 1 and 2 continue upcourt on a 2-on-1 fast break with player 3 defending. If player 1 missed the lay-up, the break starts immediately upon player 2 retrieving the rebound. Player 3 must get back on defense as quickly as possible. Players 1 and 2 should go as wide as possible upcourt. We place cones on the floor at midcourt to guide

Diagram 1

the players. As soon as 1, 2 and 3 finish, the next three players go. (See Diagrams 1 & 2)

Teaching Points: Dribble the ball as little as possible. Try to get the defense to commit to the ball before passing. Defense should try to force the offense to make a play under pressure above the foul line and not get backed up under the basket.

Three Drill Defense

Players 1, 2 and 3 start the drill the same as in the previous drill. This time when player 2 gets the ball, players 1 and 3 attempt to trap player 2 dribbling the ball upcourt alone. Player 2 should try to get around the trap and if she can't, she should keep her dribble alive, back up, switch hands on the dribble and try to get around the other side of the trap. Split the trap only if there is a wide opening. (See Diagram 3)

Diagram 2

Teaching Point: Keep the dribble alive.

Five Drill Offense

Players remain in line with players 1 and 6 each having a ball. Players 1, 2 and 3 continue as in the three drill offense, with players 4 and 5 following directly behind them. Player 4 runs and touches the opposite baseline with player 5 following and then defending player 4. Player 2 may now inbound the ball to either player 1 or 4. The ball cannot be entered past the foul-line extended. After the ball gets inbounded, players 1, 2 and 4 attack on offense with players 3 and 5 on defense. We use the cones on the floor to keep the wings wide to attack the basket from

Diagram 3

Diagram 4

Diagram 5

the proper angle (45 degrees) after reaching the foul line extended. Players 3 and 5 retreat on defense to set up a tandem; they must communicate who will take the top and who will take the bottom. As soon as they finish, the next five go. (See Diagram 4)

Teaching Points: Get the ball to the best ball handler in the middle of the floor and use the dribble to advance the ball. Find the open shooter.

Five Drill Defense

Players 1, 2, 3, 4 and 5 start as in the previous drill. This time when player 2 takes the ball out of bounds, player 3 guards 2 with players 4 and 5 denying player 1 the ball inbounds. Player 1 must get free below the foul-line extended to get the ball. Players 1 and 2 then attack the basket versus defenders 3, 4 and 5. (See Diagram 5)

Teaching Points: Keep the dribble alive. The offensive player without the ball cannot run away from her teammate. She must come back hard to the ball to help her teammate and be a receiver. She is responsible for getting open. Defense traps every pass.

These drills can also be done using groups of seven, 4-on-3 on offense and 3-on-4 on defense.

Coach Kay Yow
North Carolina State University
Raleigh, North Carolina

3-on-2 to 3-on-3

Diagram 1   Diagram 2   Diagram 3

Purpose:
To drill transition situations both offensively and defensively.

Organization:
Start out with three offensive players on the baseline and three defensive players on the foul line facing the offense. The coach is on the foul line facing the offense with the ball. To run this drill, you will need a 30-second shot clock.

1) The coach passes to any one of the offensive players (O1, O2, O3). (See Diagram 1)

Diagram 4

2) The densive player in line with that player must run and touch the baseline as the others run a fast break down the court, 3-on-2 live. (See Diagram 2)

3) On a score or turnover, the defensive team takes the ball out-of-bounds and pushes the ball the other direction before becoming the offensive team. The offense becomes defense and runs transition 3-on-3 to the other end. (See Diagram 3)

4) After a team scores or there is a turnover, those two teams are off and another two are on. (See Diagram 4)

Coaching Points:

Offensively: Stress the importance of proper spacing. Teach wings to run wide until they get to foul line extended and then cut in above the block at a 45-degree angle to the basket. If the break is stopped, don't force up a shot. Play is 3-on-3 live, and we stress the importance of screening and moving without the ball.

Defensively: Teach a tandom defense for 3-on-2. The top player stops the ball. The back player takes the first pass. As the bottom player takes the first pass, the top players must drop to defend the basket. The defense tries to make the offense make as many passes as possible, giving their third player time to catch up.

Variation:

After the offensive team scores, have them pick up full-court defense simulating a full-court press going the other direction. The other team takes the ball out as we play 3-on-3 full court.

Coach Cheryl Dozier
University at Buffalo
Buffalo, New York

Partner Fast Break

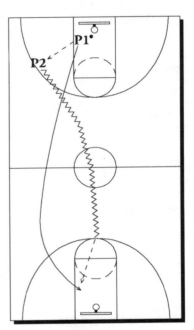

Purpose:
Incorporates conditioning, offensive transition and finishing-on-the-break skills.

Organization:
This drill requires two players.

1) Player 1 throws the ball off the glass and jumps up and rebounds the ball.

2) She then outlets the ball to player 2, who immediately pushes the ball up the middle of the floor, while player 1 flies out on the wing.

3) Player 2 will jump stop at the foul line area and pass to player 1, who is diving to the basket for a lay-up. Player 1 then rebounds the ball and outlets it to player 2.

4) Players 1 and 2 return the down the floor and perform the same action, but with player 2 passing and player 1 shooting the lay-up. This pattern continues for three more trips up and down the floor. (Therefore, the pair will sprint up and down the floor for a total of eight times.)

5) The breakdown is as follows:
   ♦ First trip: lay-up

- Second trip: jump shot
- Third trip: pass back for a jump shot
- Fourth trip: give-and-go for a lay-up

Coaching Points:

- Again, fundamentals with conditioning are the emphasis.
- Make sure the player is pushing the ball hard, with head and eyes up, good jump stops, etc.
- It is also important that rebounder sprints up the floor and gets ahead of the person handling the ball. This will help emphasize conditioning and running the floor.

Coach Duffy Burns
Cleveland State University
Cleveland, Ohio

Michigan Drill

Purpose:
To enhance the transition game with a drill that makes a player pass, catch and shoot.

Organization:
4, 8 or 12 trips, See Diagram 1
1) Player 1 passes to player 2

2) Player 2 passes to player 1

3) Player 3 sprints down the floor through the hash marks looking for the pass from player 1 to score a lay-up.

4) After player 1 passes to player 3, she must sprint and touch the baseline behind the shooter, because player 1 will be the shooter on the next trip.

Diagram 1

5) Player 2 is the rebounder and player 3 becomes the outlet.

See Diagram 2
6) Player 2 rebounds made shot and passes to player 3.

7) Player 3 passes to player 2.

8) Player 1 sprints down the floor through the hash marks looking for the pass from player 2 to score the lay-up.

Diagram 2

9) After player 2 passes to player 1, she must sprint and touch the baseline behind the shooter, because player 2 will be the shooter on the next trip.

10) Player 3 is the rebounder and player 1 becomes the outlet.

Coach Joe McKeown
George Washington University
Washington, D.C.

3/2 Olympics

Purpose:
To develop transition offense and
defense skills.

Organization:
1) Players X1, 2 and 3 attack 3-2
   against players X4 and X5.

2) X4 and X5 rebound and outlet to X6,
   then continue 3-2 full court.

3) Continue for five to eight minutes.

4) The two wings and offense become
   the defense after they shoot.

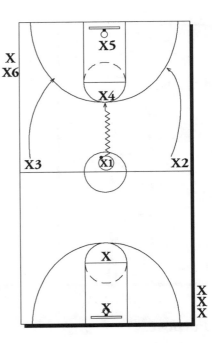

Coach Duffy Burns
Cleveland State University
Cleveland, Ohio

Perfection Drill

| Diagram 1 | Diagram 2 | Diagram 3 |

Purpose:
To enhance our transition game with a drill that makes players pass, catch, run and shoot continuously. This drill also improves concentration.

Organization:
There are five levels of perfection:
1) Full-court lay-up
2) Box-to-box lay-up
3) Same-side lay-up
4) Three-player weave — lay-up
5) Three-player weave — jumper

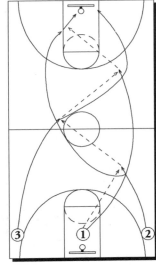

| *Diagram 4* | *Diagram 5* | *Diagram 6* |

1) Full-court lay-up (See Diagram 1)
   a) Right-hand lay-up at both ends of the floor
   b) Use alternating dribbles and try to use no more than seven dribbles total
   c) When the first player gets to half court, then the next player goes.

2) Box-to-box lay-up (See Diagram 2)
   a) Players 1 and 2 pass back and forth
   b) Call box-to-box at half court
   c) Player 1 jump stops at elbow and player 2 shoots the lay-up
   d) Player 1 rebounds the made lay-up and player 2 becomes the outlet
   e) Use no more than five passes on each trip.
   f) Players 2 and 1 pass back and forth (See Diagram 3)
   g) Call box-to-box at half court
   h) Player 2 jump stops at elbow and player 1 shoots the lay-up
   i) Next group goes.

3) Same side lay-up (See Diagram 4)
   a) Players 1 and 2 pass back and forth on the right side of the floor.
   b) Player 3 sprints down the floor through the hash marks, looking for the pass from player 1 to score the lay-up.

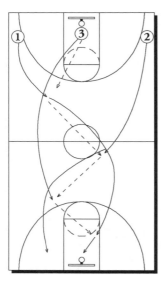

Diagram 7

c) Player 1 rebounds the made lay-up, player 3 becomes the outlet and player 2 becomes the shooter on the next trip.

d) Use no more than five passes on each trip.

e) Players 1 and 3 pass back and forth (See Diagram 5)

f) Player 2 sprints down the floor through the hash marks, looking for the pass from player 1 to score the lay-up.

g) Next group goes.

4) Three-player weave — lay-up (See Diagram 6)

5) Three-player weave —Jumper

a) Player 1 passes to player 2 and cuts behind

b) Player 2 passes to player 3 and cuts behind

c) Player 3 passes to player 1 and cuts behind

d) Player 1 passes to player 2 for lay-up

e) Player 3 rebounds made lay-up and player 1 becomes outlet

f) Player 3 passes to player 1 and cuts behind (See Diagram 7)

g) Player 1 passes to player 2 and cuts behind

h) Player 2 passes to player 3 and cuts behind

i) Player 3 passes to player 1 for lay-up

j) Next group goes

In level five, use the same procedure as used in level four, except that the shooter should jump stop on the wing for a jumper. If a jumper is missed, just follow up the miss.

Coaching Notes:
1) Every player goes at least once in each level
2) The player must score at both ends in each level
3) There can be no ballhandling or passing errors
4) Each player must use the glass on all lay-ups
5) The drill must be done at full speed
6) Everything must be perfect or the player must repeat that level.

3-on-2 Chaser

Purpose:
To develop the decision-making abilities of the point guard.

Organization:
The drill is run as a 3-on-3 with a defensive chaser. The point guard gets a 15-foot head start on the chaser who is starting on the baseline. The other two defenders are just inside their respective players two steps closer to their defensive basket. On the whistle, the point guard pushes the ball 3-on-2 with the chaser trailing the play. Communication is essential for the defense to keep the offense from scoring.

Variation:
The drill can be used as a team competition drill. Six players are needed on each team. After the first group goes, the next six players step on. The drill is then repeated. After the second group goes, the teams switch offense to defense. Score is kept throughout, with the game ending with either a predetermined possession limit or specific time allotted.

Coach Cheryl Reeve
Indiana State University
Terre Haute, Indiana

5-on-0 Weave to 3-on-2 Transition

Purpose:
This drill emphasizes advancement of the ball up the floor quickly. Points of emphasis in weave include *communication (call name of player you are passing to)*, *running ahead* when you do not have the ball, and *pass ahead* of player you are passing to in an effort to continue movement up the floor.

Diagram 1

Diagram 2

Points of emphasis in 3-on-2 include communication (defense in particular), quick inbound or outlet and advancement of the ball up the floor to put offense in good position to take advantage of "numbers;" offense takes first available good shot (goal = lay-up). Play the drill out until the offense scores or the defense secures the rebound.

Organization:
Five players begin along the baseline with the ball in the hands of the middle player (3). Player 3 will begin the drill by passing ahead to either side, in this case to player 2, and then will run behind that player to fill a lane; player 2 will then pass ahead to player 4 and fill behind 4; player 4 will then pass ahead to player 1 and fill behind 1. Player 1 will then pass ahead to player 5 who drives in for a lay-up. (See Diagrams)

The player who passes to the shooter (1) and the shooter (5) sprint back to take defensive position (tandem); three players on offense inbound/outlet and advance the ball up the floor to convert a fast-break opportunity.

Coach Charlene Curtis
Wake Forest University
Winston-Salem, North Carolina

3-on-3 Full-court Score and Defend

Diagram 1

Diagram 2

Purpose:
To improve offense and defense concepts in game conditions.

Organization:
Rules in the Backcourt:

♦ Offense may not dribble.

♦ Offense must position herself between the ball and the defender.

♦ Offense may not use screens

♦ Offense must cut on a straight (vertical) line toward the ball in order to receive a pass. Cuts may be on an angle but never horizontal.

♦ Offense may use post swim move techniques and post-up to gain advantage versus defense.

♦ Passes may not be made over the defender's head.

♦ Defense must stand within two feet of the offense in a full face denial. (Defense has her back to the ball).

1) Player 1 inbounds the ball to player 2. Player 1 is permitted to run the baseline.

Player 2 goes away then cuts back to the ball through the defender. Player 3 goes away to create good spacing. If player 2 did not get open for pass

144

from player 1, player 3 cuts back to the ball. (See Diagram 1)

2) Player 2 passes to player 3 who has cut back to the ball through her defender. Player 1 goes away to create good spacing. If player 3 did not get open for a pass from player 2, player1 cuts back to the ball. (See Diagram 2)

Rules in the Frontcourt:

♦ Offense and defense use fundamental basketball techniques for 3-on-3 basketball play.

♦ Offense is permitted to screen and dribble. (Coach may limit offense's options.)

♦ Defense uses man principles as directed by coach.

Diagram 3

♦ If offense scores, defense now becomes offense and follows backcourt rules going to the opposite basket. Offense becomes defense.

3) Player 3 passes to 1 who has cut back to the ball. Then player 1 passes to 2 who cuts back to the ball. When the ball is caught in the frontcourt, the offense may now screen and dribble. The defense plays good half-court man defense as directed by the coach. (See Diagram 3)

The goal is to score and then prevent the opponent from scoring on consecutive possessions. Drill continues until Team A or Team B scores, then successfully defends on consecutive possessions. If Team A scores then successfully defends, Team A goes out of the drill. A new three-player team steps on the court as defense versus Team B.

Benefits of Score and Defend Drill:
1) Teaches offensive players to move without the ball.
2) Teaches offensive change-of-direction moves.
3) Teaches passing and catching versus pressure defense.
4) Acts as a conditioning drill for both offense and defense.
5) Provides opportunity to teach half-court 3-on-3 offense and defense. Coach determines the half-court emphasis.
6) Emphasizes the importance of getting a defensive stop in crucial game situations.

Coach Jill M. Pizzotti
Saint Louis University
St. Louis, Missouri

Transition Drill

Diagram 1   Diagram 2   Diagram 3

Purpose:

To teach transition defense.

Organization:

1) The coach calls the name of a defensive player. (In this example, player "C".) (See Diagram 1)

2) The coach passes the ball to any one of the three offensive players on the baseline. (In this example, 2). At this time, player C sprints to the baseline and then to the defensive end of the floor while players A

and B are sprinting to the defensive end of the floor. One must guard the ball, the other the first pass. (In this example, B is guarding the ball and A takes the first pass.) (See Diagram 2)

3) Player C comes in the play as quickly as possible. (See Diagram 3)

Coaching Point:

Basically, the drill starts 3-on-2, and then becomes 3-on-3. The defenders learn to communicate. The offense learns to make quick decisions in transition. Can also run drill 4-on-4.

Coach John Ishee
Saint Louis University
St. Louis, Missouri

Defensive Transition Drill

Diagram 1   Diagram 2

Purpose:
To improve defense transition skills.

Organization:
Although this drill looks like mass confusion, it is really very simple!

1) A coach shoots up a shot and one of the players rebounds it (in this diagram, it is player 5). (See Diagram 1)

2) The player then brings the ball as quickly as possible with the dribble, two others fill the quickest lanes possible and the last player trails (that's the rebounder). (See Diagram 2)

3) The defensive team from the side cannot leave until the rebounder outlets the ball. (See Diagram 3)

Defensive Goals:
1) Stop the ball
2) Take away inside options
3) Take away all ball-side options
4) Close out/block out and give up no second shots!

Diagram 3

Coach Craig Kennedy
Auburn University
Auburn, Alabama

1-on-1 to 5-on-5

Diagram 1   Diagram 2

Purpose:

To improve 1-on-1, transition offense and defense, man advantage and disadvantage situations and half-court play and full-court play.

Organization:

 Divide the team into two squads and place them on opposite sides of the court at the center line. Set a goal of total points or a time limit for

150

Diagram 3 *Diagram 4*

this exercise. The drill can begin by a jump ball, loose ball or make it, take it.

Start out with a 1-on-1 situation. In diagram 1, player A has the ball on offense first. As soon as player 1 takes possession of the ball (rebound, turnover, score) teammate 2 comes on and goes to the outlet spot (see diagram 2). The drill is now 2-on-1 (see diagram 3). As soon as A's team gets the ball, the two teammates B and C come on. B is the outlet and C can go long (see diagram 4). The drill is now 3-on-2 (See diagram 5). When 1 and 2 get the ball, they are joined by 3 and 4 to make

Diagram 5

Diagram 6

Diagram 7

Diagram 8

Diagram 9

the drill 4-on-3 (see diagrams 6 and 7). When ABC take possession, they are joined by D and E to make the drill 5-on-4 (see diagrams 8 and 9). When 1234 get the ball, 5 joins in to make it 5-on-5 (see diagram 10).

After the 5-on-5 situation, you can stop and start over at 1-on-1 or add more players to increase the pressure by going on to a 6-on-5 situation. The drill follows with adding one player on the first change of possession, two players on the second, third and fourth possession, and add one player on the last possession.

Diagram 10

Scenes from Five-Star

CHAPTER SIX
Rebounding Drills

Coach Allison Greene
Old Dominion University
Norfolk, Virginia

Arcs and Angles

| Baseline | Wing | 3-point Circle |

Purpose:

This drill is all about physics. It is designed to improve both offensive and defensive rebounding.

Organization:

Begin with two players – one is shooting, one is rebounding. The intent is to train the eye to anticipate where a missed shot may fall. This is done by observing the following things:

1. Distance: the rebounder takes into account the distance from whence the shooter is shooting (For example, longer shots result in longer rebounds, etc.)

2. Arc: the rebounder watches the flight of the ball to observe the arc of the ball (For example, the higher the arc, the softer the shot off the rim and the closer it will fall to the rim, etc.)

3. Angle: the spot on the floor where the shot originated from is at a certain angle to the basket. If the shot misses, one can anticipate the

most likely place the rebound will occur. (For example, a missed shot on the baseline will typically bounce to the opposite baseline, or right back to the shooter, whereas a missed shot taken at a 45 degree angle will typically miss at a 45 degree angle to the other side of the key, etc.)

Close Distance

Have your team partner up and rebound for each other. The shooter should take multiple shots from varied spots on the floor. As the shooter is shooting, say 20 shots from the same distance on the right baseline, the rebounder is taking note of what that teammate's shot looks like in the air a) when it goes in the hole and b) when it misses. Eventually, the rebounder gets better at anticipating a missed shot's typical location and can move in the direction of where the ball may go. On a missed shot, the rebounder must grab the offensive board and finish the shot. This is done at game speed.

Over time, as partners are rotated and teammates rebound for all other team members, the desired result is better rebounding anticipation skills. While the more specific and individualized styles of your opponents are less familiar, one can still better approximate the most likely place a missed shot will occur. Sometimes, it is helpful for your team to take a few minutes to observe the other team's shooting styles during the time teams are casually shooting (before the structured 20 minute warm-up period). One can observe scouting films as well. Watch the players who take the most shots, in particular. In comparison to past seasons, take note of your overall offensive rebounding average to see if it increases with the implementation of this drill in practice. You will notice that the best rebounders (at all levels of the game) already utilize the above methods instinctively.

Note: These diagrams are simple examples to show where the rebounder would be in anticipation of a missed shot.

Coach J. Carol Ross
University of Florida
Gainesville, Florida

High-Low Rebounding

Diagram 1   Diagram 2   Diagram 3

Purpose:
This drill works on shooting, boxing out and rebounding in a competitive atmosphere.

Orgnization:
Divide players into two teams. They can split by first team vs. second team, posts vs. guards, younger players vs. older players, etc.

1) Each team occupies the three spots on the court. (See Diagram 1)

2) The coach throws the ball to the shooter (1) on team A. Players 2 and 3 must post and roll for the ball. (The are penalized one point if they do not.) X2 and X3 must assume defensive positions (They are penalized one point if they do not). X1 prepares to rebound on the weak side. (See Diagram 2)

3) Player 1 shoots (3-point shot unless coach restricts range for particular shooters) and follows shot. Player 3 rebounds strong side with X3 boxing out. Player 2 rebounds weak side with X2 boxing out. X2 rebounds to the weak side (see figure …) If offense rebounds, play until scored (defense matches up) or defense rebounds. If defense rebounds, outlet to manager. (See Diagram 3)

Diagram 4

4) Repeat with coach passing to team B. Team B is now on offense. (See Diagram 4)

Diagram 5

5) Drill continues alternating sides with each shooter shooting two shots before rotating. (See Diagram 5)

Coaching Points:
a) Play for four minutes, keeping time and score on the clock.

b) Scoring as follows:
Made 2- or 3-point shot: 1 point
Offensive rebound: 1 point
Defensive rebound: 1 point
Shooting foul: 1 point
Players 2 and 3 don't post/call for ball: -1 point
X2 and X3 don't defend Players 2 and 3 before rebounding: -1 point

c) Loser runs a Gator maker.

Coach Belinda "Boe" Pearman
University of Rhode Island
Kingston, Rhode Island

Monster Rebounding

Purpose:
Focus on physical play with the ability to finish the shot.

Organization:
The drill starts with the coach and three to four players at a basket.

1) The players are moving around. The coach throws the ball off the backboard, and the players scramble to gain possession of the ball.

2) The player that gets the ball tries to score against the other players — she may NOT dribble.

3) Only limited fouls are called — none in most cases.

4) After scoring, drill begins again with coach's toss.

5) The winner is the first player to score five buckets.

Coach Kay Yow
North Carolina State University
Raleigh, North Carolina

2-on-2 Rebounding

Purpose:
To drill both offensive and defensive rebounding techniques.

Diagram 1

Organization:
This drill requires 12 players and one ball. Six players are positioned at the foul line, three at each elbow facing the basket. They are on offense. The other six are positioned under the basket in two lines. They begin as the defense. Rotation of lines is based on who scores. One of the defensive lines starts the drill by making a pass to one of the offensive lines. There is no out-of-bounds in this drill. Everything is in-bounds.

Diagram 2

The ball starts in line A or B. The player passes the ball to line C or D. (The shot clock is started with 20 seconds on it when the first shot is taken.) The player in line C or D shoots as lines A and B contest shot and box out at the elbows. Play is now live regardless of whether a shot is made or missed, and all four players try to box each other out and rebound the ball. The team that rebounds the ball tries to score and play is live, 2-on-2. Both teams continue to try to box out and rebound on shots until there is a score. The team that scores fills in lines A and B. The losers go to the top, filling lines C and D. After a three-five minute time period, players in line C and D run a sprint.

Coaching Points:
1) Stress the importance of boxing out and staying with the play. Teach players to be aggressive and to go up strong.
2) Box out on short shots as well as long shots.
3) Offensively, don't be a stationary target. Move and counter the defensive box out to get to the ball.
4) This should be an intense fast-moving drill. If a foul occurs, fouling team is off and goes to line C or D and the team that was fouled is off and goes to lines A and B.

Coach Karen Hall
North Carolina A&T State University
Greensburg, North Carolina

Rebound-Outlet-Middle Drill

Purpose:
To improve rebound and outlet passing. Initiate the fast break.

Organization:
1) The rebounder outlets the ball to the player on wing. Rebounder fills right lane.

2) The outlet passes the ball to the middle player sprinting to center. Run and fill left lane.

3) The middle dribbles to the free-throw line and passes ball right to left for shooter.

OUTLET LINE

SPRINT TO MIDDLE PRIOR FOR PASS

COMES BACK FOR PASS

M

R

M
M
M

R
R
R

MIDDLE LINE

REBOUND LINE

163

Coach Kathy Warner Corbett
Oglethorpe University
Atlanta, Georgia

Team Rebounding

Purpose:
To improve team rebounding.

Organization:
O – offensive teams
X – defensive teams

1) X1 rolls ball to O1 and follows to defend O1.

2) O1 shoots upon receiving the ball.

3) Defensive team blocks out.

4) Both teams go hard for the rebound. If offense gets the rebound, they continue trying to score. Once defense gets rebound, X and O rotate one position to the right.

Coach Kevin L. Allen
West Florence High School
Florence, South Carolina

"21" Rebound Drill

Purpose:
To get players more involved in the aspect of rebounding. This employs the actions of offensive and defensive rebounding skills. This drill can be performed for a complete team or merely the post players on your team.

Organization:
Three balanced lines are established.
There are lines at each elbow and one in the middle at the free-throw line. A basketball is placed at the front of the two lines at the elbow. The middle line will not recieve a ball.

On the signal the two lines with basketballs will shoot from their line position. The middle line that does not have a ball will work for defensive rebound position to gain possession of a ball. If the individual from the middle line does get a rebound she can stick it back in for a point. When a shot is made, regardless if from the line or on a stick-back, the person that shot the ball must get a rebound and pass the ball back to her line. If the shot is missed the ball must be rebounded and put back in. Any shot made from the line position is worth 2 points. Any rebound stick-back is worth one point.

There is always going to be a player without a ball. Once the balls are shot at the beginning there is a battle for each rebound and stick-back. The first team to get to 21 points is the winner with the other two performing the extra skill of the coaches' choice while the winners sit out.

Coach Eric L. Stratman
Quincy Senior High School
Quincy, Illinois

Group Rebounding Drills

Diagram 1

Diagram 2

Purpose:

To improve team rebounding skills.

Organization:

1) *Meatgrinder Drill:* The coach shoots with the rebound rim in place. Three players on defense block out, board and outlet. Their starting positions may be varied.

   Two guards, upon seeing rebound, angle out to recieve outlet. Nonreceiving guard fills middle and non-rebounding forward fills outside. Allow fouling, but no biting.

   Two defenders wait at the opposite end to complete 3-on-2 break (see diagram 1).

Variations:

- ♦ Eliminate fast-break part of drill to emphasize the board work.
- ♦ Use 4-on-4, 5-on-5, to start the drill.

2) *Outlet Pass Drill:* Every other player in line along lane starts with a ball. The ball is put up on boards and then that player clears out to receive outlet pass.

    The next player in line rebounds the ball and clears out to the 38-foot line. A coach usually fights each rebound and outlet.

    Squad stays on the drill until 25 "good ones" are had from each side of the board (see diagram 2).

Coach Keith Holubesko
Rogers High School
Newport, Rhode Island

The Rebound Game

Purpose:

To improve defensive rebounding skills.

Organization:

The drill setup begins with three offensive players and three defensive players on the perimeter. Under the basket are three lines that are for other players in teams of three waiting to rotate in the drill. The drill starts with the coach blowing the whistle. Once the whistle is blown, the offensive players pass the ball around the perimeter while the defense works on defensive positioning only. When the whistle is blown again, the offensive player with the ball shoots. The players on defense first yell "shot" to inform their team that a shot has been taken. The second verbal is "box," which tells the defensive players to box out their offensive opponents. The game is played to five points. The first team to reach five wins. The only way to get a point is to obtain a rebound on defense. Therefore, the rotation of the drill is that the team that does not get a rebound gets out of the drill, the team that got the rebound goes to defense or stays on defense, and the team waiting comes in on offense always. Be aware that some players may cheat by running in without boxing out. If so, then take away their turn. The game is usually played until one team is left and usually they are made to run some kind of conditioner.

Coach Dave Odom
Wake Forest University
Winston-Salem, North Carolina

Rebounding Drills

Purpose:
To improve offensive and defensive rebounding skills.

Organization:
Points to remember to become a good rebounder:

Defensive Rebounding
a) When a shot goes up, find your player and make contact outside the lane
b) Make contact with the forearm, then butt
c) Knees bent with hands up and elbows out
d) Pursue the ball; be the reactor
e) Grab the ball with two hands
f) Chin the ball

Offensive Rebounding
a) Be active; go every time
b) Try to get inside your player and then block her out; if you can't get inside, get beside; if you can't do either, push her under the basket
c) Don't lean on the player blocking you out; use your feet to create space and get around
d) "Attitude is everything" – every shot is a pass to you
e) If you can't rebound the ball, tip it out to keep it alive
f) If you are fronted, sprint to the weakside on the shot

Warm-up
1) *Rim Touches:* Jump off two feet and touch the rim or a certain spot on the wall for 45 seconds, then repeat. Make sure you keep both arms high and as soon as your feet hit the floor, jump again (be a quick jumper).

Diagram 1   Diagram 2

2) *Outlet Rebounding:* Throw the ball off the boards; rebound the ball with two hands. Chin the ball then pivot to the outside and outlet the ball. Do this continuously for one minute.

Offensive Rebounding Drill
Player 1 is facing the coach, chopping her feet. The coach shoots, player 1 pivots and rebounds the ball. Players 2 and 3 must wait until the ball hits the rim. Then they go hard to the ball and try to strip it from player 1. Player 1 must make the outlet pass (see diagram 1).

Two Man Offensive Rebounding Drill
Players 1 and 2 start at elbows of free throw lane. Coach shoots and 1 and 2 go hard to the ball. They play the ball until someone scores or the ball goes out of bounds (see diagram 2).

Two-on-Two Rebounding
Two coaches are at the guard positions. Players 1 and 2 must react defensively when the ball is passed guard to guard. When a coach shoots, players 1 and 2 must block out (see diagram 3).

Rebounding Outlet Continues Drill
Player 1 passes to 2, 1 jab fakes and receives pass from 2. Player 1 throws ball to the right side of board and rebounds the ball and makes an outlet passto player 3. Player 3 passes to 4 and the drill continues. Player 1 replaces 3, 3 goes to the end of the line (see diagram 4).

Diagram 3

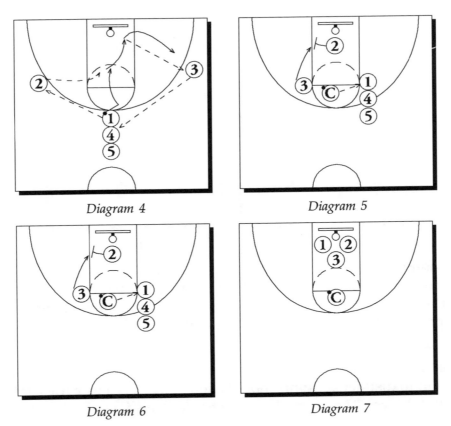

Diagram 4

Diagram 5

Diagram 6

Diagram 7

Two-on-One Drill
Coach stands at free-throw line and passes the ball to player 1 or 3. Player 2 must go opposite the pass and block. Shooter follows her shot and they play until 2 rebounds or 1 and 3 score (see diagram 5).

Toughness Drill
Players must stay in the lane, and they cannot dribble. The coach starts the drill with a shot or a pass. Players try and keep each other from scoring. Player stays in until she scores three baskets. Players keep trying to put the ball in the basket even after made shots while the other two players are contesting her. If the ball flies way out of hte lane, let it go and the coach will enter another ball with a shot immediately (see diagram 6).

Three-on-Three Rebounding
Two coaches pass the ball back and forth. The offensive players remain stationary and the defense must react on each pass. When the coach shoots, 1-2-3 must block (see diagram 7).

Diagram 8	Diagram 9

Four-on-Four Rebounding
Two coaches the ball back and forth. Offensive players can move but must stay on their side of the floor. Defense must maintain correct defensive position and block out when the ball is shot (see diagram 8).

One-on-One Close-out
Player 1 rolls the ball to 2 and then moves into defensive position with a hand up to distract 2's jump shot. Player 1 blocks out as 2 tries to follow her shot. Player 1 becomes the next shooter (see diagram 9).

Three-on-Three Rebounding
Have players slide across lane continuously. Coach will shoot the ball and player sliding will yell shot. Players sliding in the lane must go and block out player outside the lane and secure three defensive rebounds in a row. Have offense players crash the glass and each player in the lane must communicate and find a man outside the lane to box out. After three consecutive defensive rebounds, change the offense(see diagrams 10 and 11).

Diagram 10	Diagram 11

CHAPTER SEVEN

Post Player Drills

Coach Jack Miller
Rider University
Lawrenceville, New Jersey

Feeding the Post

Diagram 1

Diagram 2

Purpose:

To improve catching, reading the defense and shooting in the post.

Organization:

One passer is positioned at the right and left wing. Put four players under the basket.

1) Player 1 posts up big on the right low block showing where she wants the ball. Player C1 feeds Player 1 with a pass, forcing her to go get the ball.

2) P1 catches the ball and brings it into her chin.

3) Next, P1 will look to the middle over her right shoulder to read the imaginary defender.

4) After looking to the middle, P1 will make a post move going to the basket.

5) As P1 gets her own rebound, she outlets to C2 and reposts on the left low block.

6) P2 outlets to C1 and posts up on the right low block.

7) C1 and C2 pass into P1 and P2 forcing each to go get the ball.

8) Both P1 and P2 must "chin" the ball and look middle to read the defense.

9) After reading the defense, P1 and P2 can make a post move to the basket.

10) P1 shoots and rebounds her ball, then goes to the end of the line. P2 rebounds and outlets to C2; P3 outlets to C1.

Coaching Points:
- Player will be able to show a target hand where she wants the ball.
- Player will be able to go after the ball and bring it into her body.
- Player will be able to look middle and read the defense.
- Player will be able to perform a post move (drop step, turn around jumper, baby hook, or an up-and-under move).

Coach Jessica Smith
Bishop Hartley High School
Columbus, Ohio

Tap and Finish Drill

Purpose:
This drill is designed to strengthen both the left and right hand, rebounding and finishing skills. This drill can be used by both posts and guards.

Organization:
The player gets one ball and stands facing the backboard on the right side of the basket. The player's shoulders should be square to the backboard. To initiate the drill, begin to try one-handed taps off the backboard. If the player is having trouble with one-handed taps, try using both hands every other time. The player will tap the ball up to the backboard five times in a row. On the sixth, rip the ball down in a "Z" pattern, but make sure the player keeps the ball above her shoulders. This is done to secure the rebound and rip it down strong. She must then keep her inside elbow (on this side it will be her left elbow) up and pointed toward the center of the lane. The player will then jump and extend toward the rim and power the ball up against the backboard and through the hopp. She must use her right hand on the right side and left hand on the left side. She must not dribble! Then she will move to the other side of the rim and work on the left. The players will continue to move back and forth. As they get better, players should test themselves on how many they can do in a row without a miss or fumble.

Coach Duffy Burns
Cleveland State University
Cleveland, Ohio

Post Moves

Diagram 1

Diagram 2

Diagram 3

Purpose:
To enhance the development of the post player.

Diagram 4

Diagram 5

Organization:
1) V-cut to set man up (See Diagram 1)

2) Post up above the block (See Diagram 2)

3) Drop step, crab dribble, power move (See Diagram 3)

4) Step, shoot jumper (See Diagram 4)

5) Step through, show jumper, crossover step with or without dribble, shoot lay-up or power move (See Diagram 5)

6) Stick, then shoot the jumper (See Diagram 6)

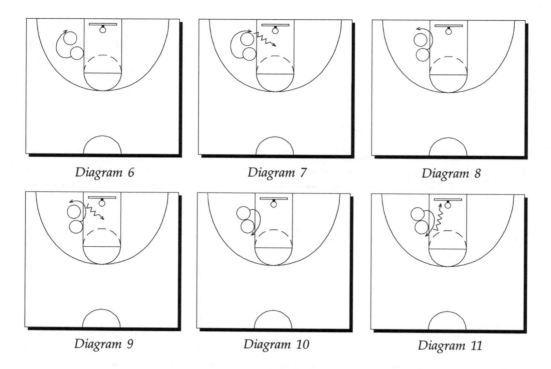

Diagram 6   Diagram 7   Diagram 8

Diagram 9   Diagram 10   Diagram 11

7) Stick through, show the jumper, crossover step with or without dribble, shoot jump hook or baby hook (See Diagram 7)

8) Reverse (Sikma) pivot and shoot jumper (See Diagram 8)

9) Reverse (Sikma) pivot, show jumper, crossover step using dribble, shoot jump hook or baby hook (See Diagram 9)

10) Reverse (Sikma) pivot and shoot jumper (See Diagram 10)

11) Reverse (Sikma) pivot, show jumper, crossover step using the dribble, shoot a lay-up or power move (See Diagram 11)

Coach Kathy Warner Corbett
Oglethorpe University
Atlanta, Georgia

Post Play/Rebounding Game

Purpose:
To improve post player's rebounding skills.

Organization:
The coach shoots. Four players fight for the rebound and try to score. The player who scores goes out and the next player in line comes in. Players keep track of their own points.

- One point per basket
- No fouls are called
- First player to score seven points wins

Coach Greg T. Collins
Dupont Manual High School
Louisville, Kentucky

Two Balls-Two Post Players

Diagram 1   Diagram 2

Purpose:

To improve catching, reading the defense and shooting in the post.

Organization:

Post players 4 and 5 each have a ball and face the backboard. Passers, players 2 and 3, are in position to receive an outlet and make an entry pass.

1) Players 4 and 5 toss the ball off the board, getting the rebound and making an outlet to the guard on their side (see diagram 1).

2) As the perimeter players make an entry pass to the post, the post players exit the lane, catching the ball and landing with a two-footed "crow hop." This allows the post to execute a post move using either foot as the pivot foot (see diagram 2).

Diagram 3   *Diagram 4*

3) Each post player then completes a post move, getting her own rebound.

4) Players 4 and 5 continue the drill by making a pass out to the opposite side and moving toward that side to receive another pass and execute another post move (see diagram 3).

5) Players continue at game speed for 1 1/2 to 2 minutes.

Variation:
♦ Add a single defender (see diagram 4) to mix up guarding the post players.

Coaching Points:
♦ Post players work on game shots at game speed.
♦ Work on a variety of moves and countermoves.
♦ Perimeter players work.

Two Balls-Two Post Players-Fan Out ⹀

Diagram 1   *Diagram 2*

Purpose:
To improve post play.

Organization:
This drill is the same as "2 ball-2 posts" except the passing.

1) After players 4 and 5 have completed their post move, they make an outlet pass to the perimeter player on their side.

2) The perimeter player will make a return pass to the post (see figure 1).

3) After catching the pass with a two-footed jump shot (crow hop) out of the lane, the post player will fan the ball out to the opposite way (see figure 2).

4) Each post will make a cut to the ball to make another post scoring move (see figure 3).

5) Repeat the passing after getting their own rebound. Continue for one minute.

Diagram

Coach Allison Greene
Old Dominion University
Norfolk, Virginia

Post Versatility

| Transition | High Post | Trail |

Purpose:

Post players are no longer limited to the blocks. In fact, to go to the next level, it is imperative that posts have a more versatile inside-out game. Scoring lay-ups in the paint cannot be the only place a post is effective. This drill implements four main scoring areas from whence a post must be able to score. The four areas are:

♦ *Transition*
♦ *High Post*
♦ *Trail*
♦ *Block*

Organization:

The post player begins at half court on one side of the floor. The passer waits at the foul line with a ball. The player runs the lane and cuts in, at game speed, to the basket. She receives the ball on the run for a lay-up. The passer rebounds. After shooting, make or miss, the post goes immediately to the opposite elbow for a jumper. The passer again rebounds.

Block   *Otherside: Transition*   *High Post, Etc.*

The post then fades back to the top of the circle and takes a three point shot in the trail position. As the passer again rebounds, the post goes to the same side low block, receives a pass, and makes a strong power move. All this time the passer is both rebounding and passing to her partner. Once the post has taken the shot on the blocks, she sprints back to half court and runs in again for a transition lay-up. Then, back to the high post. Then, the trail. Lastly, the low block again. She repeats this series until she makes a total of ten shots. The made shots can be at any or all of the spots. Once she has made ten, she sprints to the other side of the half court and runs the lane for a lay-up. She then proceeds to the opposite elbow for the same sequence at the other side. After she has made ten total shots, have her go to the free throw line. Repeat.

Coach Greg T. Collins
Dupont Manual High School
Louisville, Kentucky

Get Open: Post-up, Step, Spin and Pin

Purpose:
To improve post play.

Organization:
The offensive post player stands facing the lane will usually find herself facing the defender also. The coach or player has the ball on the wing, freethrow line extended (see diagram 1).

Diagram 1

1) The offensive post player steps with her top foot, placing it directly between the defender's feet (the step).

2) Next, the player will make an aggressive reverse pivot on the foot that was placed between the defender's feet (the spin).

3) The post player pins the defender by becoming a wide target, always keeping her hands open to the ball, her elbows out away from her body and showing her numbers to the passer.

4) As the defender attempts to get around, the offensive post player

Diagram 2

maintains contact with the defender and continues to present a wide target to the passer, always showing her numbers directly to the ball (figure B).

5) Catch the entry pass, "chin it" and pass it back. Continue for 20 to 30 seconds.

Coach Greg T. Collins
Dupont Manual High School
Louisville, Kentucky

High-Post Scoring Series

Purpose:

To improve post play.

Organization:

Post players create two lines beginning outside the lane just below the block.

Diagram 1

1) The first player does a self-toss, tossing the ball up so that it bounces around the elbow area of the lane. She follows her toss, catching it after the first bounce. She should jump stop around the elbow area, make a forward pivot and shoot a jump shot. After the first player has gone through the middle of the lane, the player in the opposite line makes the same self-toss.

2) Each player follows her shot for the rebound or gets the ball out of the net and goes to the next line.

3) The series:
♦ Jump shot (figure 1)
♦ Swing through and drive, one dribble (figure 2)

Diagram 2

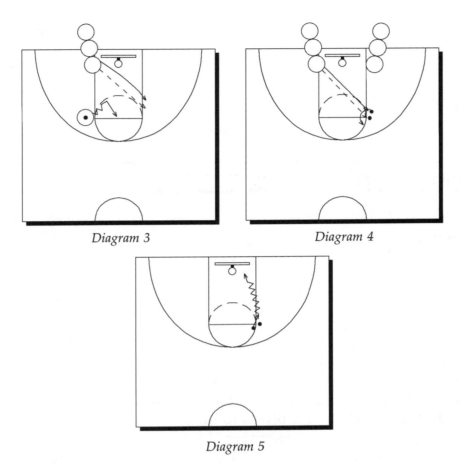

Diagram 3   Diagram 4

Diagram 5

♦ Swing through and drive, step-back jumper (figure 3)

Variation:
♦ Players can make reverse pivot after their jump stop and work on driving straight down the lane (figure 4).
♦ Reverse pivot and jump shot
♦ Shot fake and drive, using a crossover step (figure 5).

Coach Joe Ciampi
Auburn University
Auburn, Alabama

Post Bank Shots

Purpose:
To improve shooting in the low post.

Organization:
You need two chairs and two balls to run this drill. Place chairs one step away from the lane and between the block and first hash mark. Each player has one minute to shoot 12 shots. Players start at chair one with their back to the basket. Player picks up ball from the chair and pivots to the baseline and shoots a bank shot. The

Diagram 1

player rebounds her own shot and places the ball back in chair one. Player sprints to chair two and repeats action. Record the number of shots made.

Diagram 2

Diagram 3

CHAPTER EIGHT

Defensive Drills

Coach Cindy Anderson
Loyola College
Baltimore, Maryland

3-on-4 Half-court Defensive Drill

| *Diagram 1* | *Diagram 2* | *Diagram 3* |

Purpose: To improve stance, lateral movement, closeout technique and communication.

Organization:

1) The coach has the ball up top. She can pass to any of the four offensive players along the three-point line. The defensive players have to move on the pass and talk about who they have. (Diagram 1)

2) If the coach passes to O1, then X2 is closer to the ball, so she stops the ball. X4 will deny O2 and X3 will help in the middle lane. (Diagram 2)

3) If O1 passes to O2, X4 has O2 covered. (Diagram 3)

4) If O1 passes to O3, then X3 would have to get out to her.

5) X4 and X2 have to talk. If X4 takes O4, then X2 gets back to the middle of lane.

Coach Cheryl Reeve
Indiana State University
Terre Haute, Indiana

4-on-4 Ball side/Help side

Purpose:

The focus of this drill is on the basic fundamentals of man-to-man defense: ball side and help side. Points of emphasis for the drill are positioning relative to the ball, determination of the "box" rule, movement on the flight of the ball, communication, and active hands.

Diagram 1

Organization:

Have four players take offensive positions at the top of the key area about 15 feet apart and at the low wing areas on each side of the floor. Assign defenders to each offensive player. Draw either an imaginary line down the middle of the lane (which would split the court into two sides, "boxes" if you will) OR lay tape down to illustrate the point of two "boxes." This would be a good idea, especially early in the season when trying to establish the basics. The fundamental "box" rule establishes that if the ball is in a "box," then defensive players guarding players in the box should be in a denial position. If the ball is not in a box, then all defensive players in that box are in help position. Simply stated: If the ball is in your box, DENY; if the ball is not in your box, HELP.

Diagram 2

Diagram 3

Diagram 3

The player who is guarding the ball declares "ball" and takes an on the ball defensive position. On-the-ball defense points of emphasis would include the verbal call of "ball," footwork forcing the offensive player to the desired area of the floor, and active hands ready to deflect any passes. The "on-the-ball" defender's goal is to control the offensive player's movements through active hands and active feet.

The defensive players not guarding the ball must determine whether that ball is in their box or not. If so, defensive player takes a denial position on her player; if not, then she declares "help side" and should take position relative to the location of the ball first and then the player she is guarding. "Help-side" positioning would include an active stance that would enable seeing both the ball and the player being guarded by that player.

The four offensive players pass the ball on the coach's command. The coach should be looking for proper positioning of each player. Additionally, coach must demand movement *on the flight* of the ball from one player to the next, as opposed to the defense shifting after the offense receives the ball. This is crucial to maintaining good defensive positioning.

Note: Many defensive principles can be added to this drill once the basics are established. (For example, defending screens, taking charges, blocking out, etc.)

Coach Jody Conradt
University of Texas
Austin, Texas

Closeout Technique Drill

Purpose:
To improve closing-out skills

Organization:
1) When the coach slaps the ball, each player pushes hard toward the coach in a closeout position at the free-throw line. When the coach throws the pass to a manager, each person must jump to the ball in a deny position. The next line of players will repeat the same drill.

Teaching Points:
   a) Knees are bent.
   b) Hands must be below waist on the approach.
   c) Inside foot is up with the outside ankle to the corner.

Coach A.C. McCullers
Clayton College & State University
Morrow, Georgia

Defensive Progression

Diagram 1   *Diagram 2*   *Diagram 3*

Purpose:

To improve one-on-one defensive concepts.

Organization:

1) The players line up for 1-on-1 defense in two lines. The defense must roll ball to her elbow. Players in line one go first. The defensive player should close out offensive player. Retreat step on first move. Box out on shot. As a variation, the coach can limit the offensive player to a set number of dribbles. (See Diagram 1)

2) Progress to 2-on-2. The players cross pass (or roll) ball to start. The emphasis is on close out. The players play screen-and-roll (hedge screens). Be sure the players cut the cutter and deny flash. Players should also watch "Ball-You-Man" spacing (one pass away). (See Diagram 2)

3) Progress to 3-on-3. The stresses are the same as 2-on-2. Add help and recover and rotation on baseline drives. Work on post defense. (See Diagram 3 and Diagram 4)

4) Progress to 4-on-4 shell. Work on all defensive principles (See Diagram 5):
   a) close out
   b) retreat steps
   c) help & recover
   d) cut the cutter
   e) hedge on screens
   f) deny the flash
   g) box out on screens
   h) rotate on drive
Coach should stress offensive moves and techniques!

5) Progress to 5-on-5. Run full offense vs. defense. Stress help on lobs to the post. Taking off changes. (See Diagrams 6, 7 and 8)

Coaching Tip:
   Position post at different postions.

Diagram 4   Diagram 5   Diagram 6

Diagram 7   Diagram 8

Coach Jill M. Pizzotti
Saint Louis University
St. Louis, Missouri

Defensive Slide/Dive Drill

Purpose:
To teach proper first-step footwork on defense.

Diagram 1

Diagram 2

Organization:
1) Player A is in a defensive stance. The coach rolls a ball to the block. A slides to the block (with outside foot), picks the ball up and throws a chest pass back to the coach. (The coach has already rolled the second ball to the other block.) (See Diagram 1)

2) Player A slides block to block passing balls back to the coach. After 15-20 seconds, the coach rolls a ball toward the sideline. A sprints, dives to save the ball and passes it up to B, who has sprinted toward A calling for the ball. (See Diagram 2)

3) During this drill, the second player in line (B), must call Left or Right, which helps player A know which foot to step with toward the block. Players have a tendency to bring their feet together before taking the first step.

Coach Kevin Chaney
Solono Community College
Suisun City, California

Defensive Slides

Purpose:
To increase change-of-direction speed and push-off strength for better defensive slides.

Organization:
Players start in the middle of the key on the whistle. Defense slides lane line to lane line. Group goes until all do drill correctly. On whistle, next three players sprint out and resume on ball stance. Short choppy steps, correct hand positioning are to be focused on. Don't allow players to bring feet together. Everyone goes three times. They must change location in key each time. On each change of direction, hand positioning switches as well. Eyes of players should be on coaches with heads up.

Coach Jody Conradt
University of Texas
Austin, Texas

Full-Court Zig-Zag

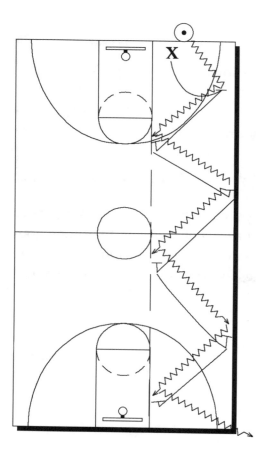

Purpose:
To improve full-court pressure

Organization:
1) The offense goes side to side, bringing the ball up the court. Early-on offense goes 3/4 speed. Defense works on technique.

Variation: Offense dribbles two balls.

Teaching Points:
a) Defense plays nose on the ball and backside to opposite baseline
b) Slide down, don't run.
c) No hands early — Defense should wait for offense to give it to them
d) Don't take it — Cut the drive off, but don't chest.

Coach Kay Yow
North Carolina State University
Raleigh, North Carolina

Help and Recover to 3-on-3 Live

| Diagram 1 | Diagram 2 | Diagram 3 |

Purpose:

This drill teaches players to help and recover. It also teaches proper defensive rotations.

Organization:

This drill requires six players, one coach, two balls and one manager. Players are positioned in shell defense spots (offense and defense in both corners and offense and defense on right wing). The coach is on the left wing and the manager is under the basket. Players rotate from offense to defense.

1) The ball starts with the coach, who passes to player 1. On the pass, defensive players adjust (similar to shell drill). (See Diagram 1)

2) Player 1 passes to 2. Again, defensive players adjust. (See Diagram 2)

3) The ball is skip-passed back to the coach. The coach drives right requiring X1 to help stop penetration. The coach then drives left re-

Diagram 4

quiring X3 to help stop penetration. (See Diagram 3)

4) The coach passes to player 3, who penetrates the baseline. For the sake of the drill, X3 allows 3 to beat her. (See Diagram 4)

5) On the penetration, X2 slides over to help and X1 drops.

6) Player 3 tries to pass across baseline to 2. X1 knocks the ball out-of-bounds to the manager, and the coach throws a "live" ball to 1.

7) Play is live (3-on-3).

Coaching Points:
♦ Good communication between players.
♦ Give early help and recover quickly.
♦ Players helping must have good body position in order to prevent the coach from getting to the basket. If the player's body position is too open, the coach will have a direct path to the basket.
♦ Help on the baseline should occur outside the lane line, otherwise it has arrived too late.
♦ The ball needs to move quickly. This hould be a very fast-paced, intense drill.

Variation: Trap the ball handler on the baseline.

Coach David Glass
Virginia Commonwealth University
Richmond, Virginia

Progressive Defensive Drills

| Diagram 1 | Diagram 2 | Diagram 3 |

Purpose:

To develop players' defensive strategy and man-to-man concepts, step-by-step.

Organization:

This is a progressive defensive drill that covers (1) wing deny, (2) defense on the ball, (3) guarding the dribble, (4) reacting to a pass that has been made, (5) help-and-recover technique, (6) live one-on-one defense, and (7) blocking out and rebounding. This is an excellent drill because it helps to develop many good defensive habits and is a good defensive conditioning drill. In this drill you must work very hard at the defensive end of the court for several minutes.

1) WING DENY: The drill starts with a defender guarding an offensive player on the wing. A passer attempts to complete a pass to the offensive player who must move to get open on the wing. We teach the defensive player to be in a position up the passing line approximately

Diagram 4

Diagram 5

three feet off the offensive player. The defense must successfully prevent the offensive player from receiving the ball for a count of five seconds, one time. (See Diagram 1)

2) ON-THE-BALL STANCE: Now we do this drill again; however, if the pass can be made to the offensive player, we do so and stop! Check the defensive stance and the position of the feet. We do not allow middle penetration so we want to see that the defensive player is positioned to force the ball to the baseline. (See Diagram 2)

3) GUARDING THE DRIBBLE: The drill begins again with the wing deny and if the pass can be made then we pass the ball. We do not stop the drill when the offensive player catches the ball, rather we allow her to take two hard dribbles and then she must pick up the ball. Once the defense stops the ball, we want the defense to get tight to the offensive player, chest-to-chest, and to cross her hands and mirror the ball. If the offense was able to penetrate to the middle of the floor, then the defensive player must do three push-ups. Remember that we do not want to allow middle penetration, so if this happens in any drill during practice, the player will automatically do three push-ups. We also like a lot of talk with our defense so we teach them to call out,"dead, dead, dead" to let the other defensive players know that the offensive player has used the dribble option and we want to deny all passes. (See Diagram 3)

4) JUMPING TO THE BALL: In our next step, we want to get our players in the habit of moving in the direction of the ball as a pass is made. We call this "jumping to the ball." We start our drill all over again and once we get to the dead-ball situation, we then have the offensive player make a pass back out to the coach. Now the defensive player must jump to the ball. The offensive player will attempt to make a face cut, that is to cut between the ball and the defensive

player. We want to always maintain a ball-you-man relationship on defense and never allow the player being guarded to cut between the player and the ball. As the offensive player starts to make a face cut, the defensive player will be in a position to bump the cutter and not allow the face cut to happen. We stop the drill after the defender bumps the cutter and gets back into a good stance to deny the pass back to the offensive player on the wing. (See Diagram 4)

5) HELP AND RECOVER: As we stated earlier, this a progressive drill, so we start over. The defensive player now must deny the pass to the wing, get in to a good on-the-ball defensive stance if the ball is caught on the wing, force the ball toward the baseline and force a dead-ball situation, jump to the ball on a pass and maintain a ball-you-man relationship, bump any attempted face cut and return to a good wing-deny defensive stance. At this point, during the wing deny, the coach will start to make a ball-side drive to the basket. Our defender should now see the drive and make a move to help our defense by stopping the ball. When the defender forces the coach to stop the dribble move and pass the ball back out to the offensive player on the wing the defender must recover back to the ball, under control, by using a closeout step. We call this a "help-and-recover" move. At this point, this becomes a live one-on-one drill. Once a shot is taken, the defense must block out and sprint to recover the rebound. (See Diagram 5)

This is a great drill to use throughout the year. We use it in preseason to teach defensive technique and we use it during the season to reinforce good defensive habits. We encourage our players to work very hard in this drill and to be very vocal. We want each of them to do it correctly one time. We have found that we get more out of this drill and it is more competitive than spending five or 10 minutes of station work doing a wing-deny drill. This is also a drill that players can do in the off-season to improve their defensive skills.

Coach Jody Conradt
University of Texas
Austin, Texas

1-on-1 Wing Drill

Purpose:
To improve 1-on-1 defense

Organization:
1) The offensive player cuts to the wing. Receiving the pass from the coach, the player goes to a 1-on-1 situation (2 dribbles max).

Teaching Points:
a) Deny Entry
b) Force the player to the corner
c) Make offense catch as far out as possible.
d) React straight back on jab step; approach top foot-back foot.

Coach Kevin Chaney
Solono Community College
Suisun City, California

Rip Throughs Defensive Drill

Diagram 1   *Diagram 2*

Purpose:

To develop quicker change of direction on the rip-through. To contain penetration and reduce chances of being beaten off the dribble. It also helps develop lateral change-of-direction movement.

Organization:

Offense can rip through and jab from the triple-threat position only. The defense must quickly shift to the ball trying to keep their heads on the ball. Go 10 seconds and then rotate. You can rip through on the whistle or let the players play independently.

Coach Kristy Curry
Purdue University
W. Lafayette, Indiana

Triangle Defensive Drill

Purpose:
To teach defensive positioning.

Organization:
Player D passes to player A and closes out on A. Player D then gets in defensive position. Player A tries to drive by and score; if she can't, then player A passes to B. Defense jumps to the ball and denies A. Player B passes to C. Player D opens and sprints to midline. Then player D denies A's flash cut.

Coach Kevin Chaney
Solono Community College
Suisun City, California

Help for the Lob/the Skip

| Diagram 1 | Diagram 2 | Diagram 3 |

Purpose:

To improve peripheral vision from the help position and improve the reaction to the pass. Must move quickly while the ball is in the air.

Organization:

Divide players into teams of three. Player 1 delivers the lob, player 2 is the weakside shooter or penetrator, and player 3 is the help defender. To work on lob, don't use help defense. Player 3 passes to lob or skip. Defender must defend the lob or steal the skip, or be there when it's caught. After a steal, rotate a new "3" on to the court. When it's their turn again, they'll play different spots. Repeat till all have gone and played all spots. Let the players communicate who will play where. This teaches them to talk before their turn. When the whistle blows they sprint to their new positions.

Coach John Ishee
Saint Louis University
St. Louis, Missouri

X-Out Drill

| Diagram 1 | Diagram 2 | Diagram 3 |

Purpose:
To develop 1-on-1 offense and defense. Improve outlet passing.

Organization:
1) This drill starts with two single-file lines at and behind the baseline. (See Diagram 1)
2) The player with the basketball (B) rolls the ball to the top of the key. She then touches the opposite black before closing out to defend the player that vacated there (player line #1). Block to retrieve the basketball at the top of the key.
3) The player in line 1 must square up in a triple-threat position before trying to shoot or drive.
4) The offensive player with the basketball keeps possession as long as she comes up with the ball, whether that's from an offensive rebound or from beating her opponent 1-on-1 to the basketball. (See Diagram 2)

5) Once the defensive player gets possession of the ball, she makes an outlet pass to the coaches stationed above the three-point arch. If possession changes due to a made basket, then the defense becomes the offense. Offense then goes to play defense.

6) Defensive player gets the ball, clears the basket and the lane area. The offensive layer becomes the defender and pressures the outlet pass. (See Diagram 3)

Coach Eric Stratman
Quincy Senior High School
Quincy, Illionois

Group Defensive Drills

Diagram 1

Diagram 2

Purpose:
To improve overall defensive skills.

Organization:
1) *One-on-One:* This drill can be played from any spot on the floor, the three most common places are shown in diagram 1. Start ball within shooting distance and defender close. Defenders can either play with towel around their necks or with hands held behind their backs.

The offensive player works on her footwork as well as the defensive player. Each offensive player executes each of the following plays:
♦ Fake shot and drive
♦ Fake shot, fake drive, shoot
♦ Rocker step and go
♦ Crossover step and go

Diagram 3   Diagram 4

2) *Two-on-Two:* Offensive player passes to her partner and sets pick and rolls to basket. Defense works on jump switches. While guarding situation shown in diagram 2, drill should also be practiced with guard-forward starting setup.

3) *Three-on-Three, Half Court (can also be started at the endline):* Middle player has ball and dribbles. The drill begins with a double high pick-and- roll and continues with three-on-three. Drill's emphasis is on jump switching and checking out on defensive rebounding (see diagram 3).

Variation:
♦ Begin with all three wide and pass and from middle player who then either picks for the player she passes to or picks away.

4) *Three-on-Three, Full Court:* Full-court 3-on-3 drill starting with ball out-of-bounds. First pass may not be past free-throw line extended and defense may two-time the receivers (see diagram 4).

5) *Three-on-Two, Two-on-One Drill:* Begins with squad in three lines at the end of the court and two players at the other end waiting to defend. Play begins as a normal 3-on-2 fast-break drill. However, when two defenders get the ball at the far end, they come back on attack against the original middle man on a 3-on-2 break.

Variation:
♦ Set time clock at four minutes and make squad get 25 baskets in the time.

Diagram 5

6) *Continuous Three-on-Two Drill:* Starts with two players at each end of the floor on defense. The first pass is from the coach to front player in line (1). Players C and D go down the court with player 1 in 3-on-2 working against A and B. If they score against A and B, defenders take ball out and pass to first player in other line (2) and join her on break. Defenders are next two players in line at far end. If there is no score, players rebound, clear and release to break. After players A and B leave the court, the next two players in line 2 take their place on defense (see diagram 5).

Variation:

♦ Set clock at 4:30. Squad must score 25 baskets (kept on board) before horn goes off. Laps for failure and drills run until they are successful.

Coach Greg T. Collins
Dupont Manual High School
Louisville, Kentucky

Stop, Charge and Contest

Diagram 1

Diagram 2

Purpose:
The objective of this drill is to teach post players how to be an effective help defender

Organization:
Three players start outside the three-point line and the post player is in the lane directly in front of the basket.

1) The coach begins the drill by passing to player 1. She immediately drives hard to the basket as if she beat her defender on the baseline side. The post defender must stop the ball outside the lane (see figure 1).

2) As soon as O1 is stopped, she passes to O2 at the top of the key. Player 2 drives straight to the basket. The post defender recovers into a defensive position in front of the ball and takes a charge (see diagram 2).

Diagram 3

3) As player 2 charges and the defender takes the charge, player 2 passes out to player 3 outside the three-point line. The defender's challenge is to get off the floor and contest the three-point shooter (see figure 3).

Player 3 goes to player 2's position after completing the action, player 2 goes to player 1's position, and player 1 goes to the end of the line or becomes the next defender. The post defender becomes player 3 on offense.

Coaching Points:

♦ When taking a charge, players must not put their hands down to brace the fall. They might injure their wrists.

♦ Teach players to contest shots or to attempt to block shots in such a way that they can still blockout for rebounding position.

CHAPTER NINE
Basketball Miscellanea

Coach Matt Masiero
Director, Five-Star Women's Basketball Camp
Robert Morris College
Pittsburgh, Pennsylvania

Setting Good Habits

20 SMALL (PRACTICE) DETAILS (HABITS) THAT MAKE A BIG DIFFERENCE
MAXIM: IF YOU DO IT IN PRACTICE, YOU'LL DO IT IN THE GAME!

The following practice guidelines were designed by me in July of 1997, while I was teaching the Team Defense Station at the Five-Star Boys' Basketball Camp, Pitt. IV session. It was during my instruction of the 'Shell Defense' that I began to notice most campers were demonstrating small, poor practice habits that had long frustrated me as a coach. It also reminded me of the numerous players that I have coached throughout the years that revealed the same idiosyncrasies. In relief of this frustration I decided to create this list.

In the list of 20 details, I first point out the problem (turnover), then submit a recommendation (steal) and finally an example of what I mean. You will notice I make no reference to concrete fundamental skills such as passing/catching techniques (target zone), dribbling techniques (dribble w/head up) and/or shooting techniques (being balanced). I have purposely steered away from addressing such aspects of the game because I believe numerous coaches before me have done a tremendous job of rectifying the problem through various drills. I do however, address aspects of practicing passing/catching, dribbling and shooting such as when, where, how and what type that I believe are beneficial and critical to improve both the team and individual.

As a player/coach you may observe none, some or all of these practice habits in yourself or players, but at least this list will hopefully give you a reference for what to reflect upon. Another reason I developed this list is to help both players and teams improve through discipline, hard work and responsibility. If it helps one player/team to improve their overall practice habits then I will be happy, but if it helps them develop such "life skills" as good decision making and problem solving, discipline, hard work, communication, organization and responsibility, then the list has truly served its purpose.

Remember what Coach John Wooden once said: "I am a teacher of life first, then a coach, whatever that is." This philosophy is something we as coaches should all adopt and I believe this list can help us become a "teacher of life" by developing our players' critical and creative thinking skills through basketball.

Before you review the list, as an introduction I would like to give you an example of what the list is truly trying to accomplish. This example is one of a critical and creative thinking nature and has been implemented into my coaching practice.

- **TURNOVER** – *Limited Critical & Creative Thinking Skills:* Players often go along and do the norm.

- **STEAL** – *Expanded Critical & Creative Thinking Skills:* Players need to enhance their critical and creative thinking skills during practice, by evaluating, assessing and analyzing every aspect of the game that requires them to solve problems and make decisions.

- **EXAMPLE:** When any practice drill begins, rather than question a coach's authority, merely inquire about his or her philosophy and style/structure, so you can appreciate that point of view. My philosophy emphasizes the development of attitudes and dispositions that can be transferred into other situations. For example, players should try to transfer all possible knowledge/skills learned on the basketball court such as: discipline, hard work, responsibility, organization and communication to other contexts such as the classroom or job. Players should put as much effort and hard work into submitting a successful English term paper or becoming the best manager possible as they would improving their jump shot.

1 **Turnover.** *Lack of Hustle:* At the start of each drill, inbetween drills and during breaks.

Steal. *Hustling:* Time is crucial! Although it may seem so, practice doesn't last that long and time should not be wasted. Get there and get to work!

Example: During practice there are too many aspects to cover and time cannot be wasted in between or on one drill.

2 **Turnover.** *Nongame Condition Pre- & Post-Practice:* Certain shots taken or dribbling around during pre-practice, between drills and/or after practice that waste time and do not improve your game. Not working on your weaknesses.

Steal. *Game Condition Pre- & Post-Practice:* Again, time is crucial, so make use of pre- and post practice time to improve your shooting and dribbling from different areas of the floor. In between drills put the ball down and get to the next drill. Work on your weaknesses.

Example: Taking half-court shots or dribbling between the legs in one area is not a game-like condition; focus the time to work on the weak areas of shooting and game conditioning dribbling.

3 **Turnover.** *Wasted Drills Offensive & Defensive:* Because the drill is either offensive or defensive in nature, the offense and/or defense tends to go through the motions, especially when it is a 5-0 drill.

Steal. *Productive Offensive & Defensive Practice:* This is extra time and the perfect opportunity to work on both the offensive/defensive ends of the floor. Make the offense/defense work harder and improve.

Example: Develop the disposition of creativity and visualization. Practice the team's offensive and defensive philosophy when involved in drills of the opposite intent. When going 5-0 practice hard and pretend the offense or defense is present.

4 **Turnover.** *Blending Skills In Drills:* Only working on one skill for that specific drill.
Steal. *Many Skills In All Drills:* There are various skills that can be worked on and preexist in the drills, they just need more practice.
Example: Develop the attitude and disposition of flexibility. When a drill is primarily designed to improve shooting, remember that chances are a rebound must be taken down and a pass must be made in order for the next player to shoot. Work on all three phases of the game.

5 **Turnover.** *Lack of Attention/Focus:* Not listening or focusing on what is being taught during drills or when reviewing an opponent's scouting report.
Steal. *Familiarity with All Positions:* Learn all positions on the floor, all aspects of the drill and the opponent's tendencies.
Example: Keep eye contact on the coach and what is happening during drills at all times. Make sure to be familiar with what your opponent is going to do. If possible, sub in for teammates of a different position.

6 **Turnover.** *Talking & Listening:* There is a time when to ask questions and a time to be quiet and listen.
Steal. *Timing:* During the explanation of drills strategically pick the opportune time to ask questions.
Example: Do not talk while on the sideline/baseline during a drill. Develop an open mind to what the coach is saying even though you may not initially agree. Once the coach is finished explaining, then it is the right time to ask questions.

7 **Turnover.** *Passing & Catching:* Making a poor pass a good catch.
Steal. *Catching & Passing:* Step to receive all passes and catch them all 2-handed by moving the body in position. Make crisp 1- and 2-handed passes with your outside hand and away from the defense.

Example: Do not try to catch passes 1-handed by trying to slap the ball. Do not stand still waiting to receive a pass. Remember, a steal or pickoff is catching someone's bad pass. Lastly, do not always pass 2-handed and across the body where the defender could be.

8 **Turnover.** *Lack of Concentration Shots:* Missing open shots close to the basket when there is no defender.

Steal. *Concentration Shots:* Focus on making the easy, open shots in all drills, especially with no defenders.

Example: When involved in drills such as the 5-man weave, focus on finishing lay-ups.

9 **Turnover.** *Making Excuses & Being A Spectator:* Taking the easy way out of responsibility and watching the game take place.

Steal. *Being Responsible & A Participant:* "Don't tell me the sea is rough, just bring the ship in." Don't think someone else will do it. Be the one who steps up and initiates the action.

Example: When coach needs a player for any drill, be the one who steps up and initiates the drill.

10 **Turnover.** *No I In Team:* Supposedly there is no (I) individual within the team.

Steal. *I Within Team:* True, that no individual is greater than the team, but the sum of each individual player can be greater than the team as a whole.

Example: If each individual is accountable, takes the responsibility of developing his or her game and makes a contribution, then the team will be much stronger, as opposed to letting teammates do the job.

11 **Turnover.** *Logical/Predictable Passing & Catching:* Players tend to throw passes that are logical and predictable. They also tend to catch passes facing the direction the ball came from. **Steal.** *Illogical/Unpredictable Passing & Catching:* Make passes that the defense can't anticipate. Pass away from the next area anticipated. Catch the ball and be facing the basket so the defense doesn't know what the next move is.

Example: When the ball is passed from the wing most players have a tendency to catch looking at the passer. They should catch facing the basket in triple-threat (basketball) position. This forces the defense to have to defend three possibilities as opposed to one.

12 **Turnover.** *Non-Basketball Positioning:* Players always stand flat-footed and straight up. **Steal.** *Basketball Positioning:* Be bent down and always on the balls of the feet. Be on the move.

Example: When defending, shooting, passing, catching, dribbling and/or rebounding being in a slightly bent position allows for easy movement. Standing straight up only wastes time, because in order to move you must bend down.

13 **Turnover.** *Perimeter/Post Dominate:* Teams and players tend to favor one area of the floor. **Steal.** *Perimeter/Post Equality:* Distribute the ball to both areas of the floors equally. Balance the offense.

Example: When passing around the perimeter make a rule that every third pass should touch a post player's hands. If passing high to low post make sure a pass reaches the perimeter every few passes.

14 **Turnover.** *Blindness:* Players who don't use the backboard when shooting at an angle and around the basket.

Steal. *Corrected 20/20 Vision:* Make use of the backboard when shooting at an angle and around the basket.

Example: Get in the habit of using the backboard to help improve shooting percentage and finishing the shot.

15 **Turnover.** *Succumbing To Screens:* Allowing a screen to be set.
Steal. *No Screens:* Don't allow the screen to be set and give up once it is.

Example: When playing defense try and not allow the offense to set a screen. If they do, execute your team's philosophy and don't fight through chest-to-chest, giving up once contact is made.

16 **Turnover.** *Letting Mistakes Dominate:* Giving up on the play after a mistake is made.
Steal. *Dominating Mistakes:* Develop the attitude of risk taking toward mistakes. Don't give up because of a brief failure.

Example: When a bad pass is thrown and the opponent steals the ball, get back on defense instead of sulking about it.

17 **Turnover.** *Tangibles:* Anybody can shoot, dribble and pass.
Steal. *Intangible:* Do the small things that make a big difference on both the offensive and defensive ends of the floor.

18 **Turnover.** *Poor Shot, Pass & Dribble Selection:* Using poor judgment and forcing shots, passes and dribbling.
Steal. *Smart Shot, Pass & Dribble Selection:* Knowing the location, game situation and what is going on during the game is crucial.

Example: If the team is up five up with 10 seconds left in the game, there is no need to shoot a 3-point shot, pass to a teammate who is double teamed or dribble through traffic to the basket.

19
Turnover. *1-2-3-4-5 Numbering Player's System:* Players have become so used to what number they are labeled that they try to develop their game according to it.

Steal. *Just Being A Basketball Player:* Develop a game that is conducive to all positions on the floor. Practice drills/skills that with help improve the total game.

Example: If you only practice shooting from the perimeter because of the 2 label, then you will be hard-pressed to drive to the basket, post up if necessary or run the team.

20
Turnover. *Poor Stretching:* Just going through the motions when warming up and stretching.

Steal. *Smart Stretching:* Go through the whole routine before and after workouts.

Example: Avoid doing just one stretch for a short period of time. Do a few different stretches, 3 X's for each body part and use a 10-second count as a standard.

Coach Stephanie V. Gaitley
St. Joseph's University
Philadelphia, Pennsylvania

Hawks' Playbook: The Mental Game

Exercises for Getting to Know Your Players and Developing Team Chemistry

A great deal of our success at St. Joseph's has to do with our commitment to our players off the court. We want to know what they think and how they feel. This information is critical in developing the makeup of our team. We feel it is important to know our players' strengths and weaknesses both on the court and off. If the players realize that you are committed to them as people, they will be more committed to you as well.

Hawk Hoop Question of the Day:

It is 1 o'clock in the morning. You are on your way back to St. Joe's and your car breaks down on the Schuykill Expressway (76). We have practice at 7 in the morning. List the player you would call first, second, third, etc.. (Note: Each player has an equal opportunity to help you.)

1._____

2._____

3._____

4._____

5._____

6._____

7._____

8._____

9._____

10._____

11._____

12._____

13._____

⇨ This exercise gives us an opportunity to see who they rely off the court. Are there similarities to who they rely on when on the court?

Hawk Hoop Question of the Day:

You are on your way to the playground to play a game of pickup. Which four of your follow Hawks do you take with you?

1. _____

2. _____

3. _____

4. _____

Why?

⇨ This exercise allows us the opportunity to see who the players want to play with and why?

Hawk Inquiry: "Getting to Know Me"

A. Family

B. Stengths

C. Weaknesses

D. What would you like people to know about you?

⇨ We use this exercise to quiz their fellow teammates on how well they know each other. We feel it is critical to our success that we are all committed to each other in order to be committed to a common goal.

Hawk Inquiry: "Who am I?"

1. What do you like most about yourself?

2. What do you like least about yourself?

3. What one person do you trust the most?

4. Who do you turn to when you need help?

5. What is your favorite part of basketball?

6. What part of practice do you dislike? Why?

7. What would you do differently if you were the head coach?

8. What do you want to do following graduation?

9. What is your purpose in life?

⇨ This exercise gives you an opportunity to find out more about your players. This is highly important when developing team chemistry.

Hawk Inquiry: "Knowing Our Roles"

Please list the top three in each category.

Rebounding:

    A. Offensive

      1. _____

      2. _____

      3. _____

    B. Defensive

      1. _____

      2. _____

      3. _____

Foul Shooting:

      1. _____

      2. _____

      3. _____

Three-Point Shooting:

      1. _____

      2. _____

      3. _____

Defense:

    A. On the Ball

      1. _____

      2. _____

      3. _____

B. Off the Ball (help)

1. _____

2. _____

3. _____

Leaders:

1. _____

2. _____

3. _____

Most Likely to Draw a Foul:

1. _____

2. _____

3. _____

Competitors:

1. _____

2. _____

3. _____

Abilty to Drive to the Basket:

1. _____

2. _____

3. _____

Players You Can Count on, Regardless of the Score:

1. _____

2. _____

3. _____

⇨ This exercise gives us an opportunity to see if the players think the same way that the coaches think. We all need to be on the same page come game time.

Coach Royce Chadwick
Stephen F. Austin State University
Nacogdoches, Texas

Using a Video Grading System

Throughout my coaching career, we have used this grade sheet to break down our team defense and offense. It has been very good to us as we have identified players' strengths and weaknesses with this system. It allows us to play our strengths while we work on developing our weaknesses.

The original grade sheet was much more simple. Due to our Run and Jump defense, we have added additional categories. If you believe strongly in zones, which we play sparingly at SFA, you will need to adjust our categories. This sheet is our standard, but could be altered to custom fit any program.

The basic postivies and negatives are as follows:

POSITIVES
1. Great motivational tool
2. Tanglible, on-paper grades
3. Cut & dried for players, parents and personnel
4. Points out strengths
5. Points out deficiencies
6. Aids in picking starting players
7. Develops consistency with play

NEGATIVES
1. Takes time
2. Good video person is imperative
3. Does not measure everything happening on the court

The grades are determined by a series of positives and negatives. We try to set our own players up to have a positive score by making many

234

positive categories worth more than one point, while the negative categories (except turnovers) are all only worth one point.

Breakdown

Positive Categories

Defensive Help (+2): In our help side defensive philosophy, any player who helps out a beaten teammate by leaving and stopping a driving player.

Offensive Rebound (+2): When a team rebound occurs, I give the credit to the player who was working to get the board as it was deflected out-of-bounds, or tied up, etc.

Defensive Rebound (+2): same as "Offensive" rebound.

Assist (+2)

Steals (+2)

Taking a Charge (+3): The only three-point nonscoring opportunity.

Basket Made (+2): Can be a +3 if a 3-pointer is made.

Blocked Shot (+3)

Free Throws Made (+1): Possibly should be +2 or +3 as poorly as some percentages appear.

Loose Ball Recovery (+1): The steal goes to the player who deflects the ball or creates the loose ball opportunity. This category is for the player who actually ends up with the loose ball.

Positive Categories (cont.)

Screen/Basket (+1): The player who sets a screen which leads to a basket.

Hustle (+1): Dive on the floor, dive out-of-bounds.

Deflection (+1): On defense, deflecting a pass or dribble that does not result in a steal.

Scoring-Area Pass Made (+1): A pass that should have been an assist, but the basket was missed.

Transition Pass Ahead (+1): A pass up the floor to create our fast break.

> Analysis of a team and players is often one of the most difficult tasks we face. This grading system can be very useful in breaking down potential problem areas.

Negative Categories

Turnovers (-2): The only negative which is valued -2.

Not rotating full court(-1): Our run and jump defense requires reading and rotating. Failure here results in a -1.

Missed shot, first half (-1)

Missed shot, second half (-1): Two boxes ensure that there is enough space for all marks.

Missed free throw (-1)

Not back on defense (-1): The player's opponent beats her down the floor.

Scoring Area Pass (-1): The player that is being guarded by your player caught the ball in an area in which she should have scored.

Deflected Pass (-1): A pass which your player made was deflected, but did not result in a turnover.

Beaten on a Screen (-1): Improper defensive guarding of a screen situation.

Not Having Hands Up (-1): Especially for zone coaches.

Not Contesting the Shot (-1): Each shot by our opponent should be taken with our player's hands high in the sight line.

Negative Categories (cont.)

Not Blocking Out (-1): Your player was not blocked off the board.

Not Overplaying (-1): Ballside players without the ball should be denied.

Influence Cut Off Baseline (-1): We influence the baseline. Any player who gets beat off the dribble to the middle or allows the ball handler to penetrate the paint-area baseline.

Not Going to the Boards (-1): Offensive rebounders who do not crash...HARD.

Not Helping in the Halfcourt (-1): Help-side players who fail to rotate over and stop penetrating dribblers in half-court sets.

"O" Execution Lapse (-1): Poor execution on offense.

No Ball Pressure (-1): Lack of defensive pressure on a dribbler, passer or dead player.

Defensive Lapse (-1): Anything on defense we want to emphasize for the day (slide step, hands on ball, see ball - see player, stance, etc.)

Offensive Lapse (-1): Failure to run the offensive set.

Basketball Miscellanea

LADYJACK BASKETBALL

Stephen F. Austin State University

Head Coach Royce Chadwick

GRADE SHEET

		Player #1	Player #2	Player #3	Player #4	Player #5	Player #6	Player #7	Player #8	Player #9	Player #10	Player #11	
Defensive Help	+2												+2
Offensive Rebounds	+2												+2
Assists	+2												+2
Steals	+2												+2
Taking A Charge	+3												+3
Baskets Made	+2												+2
Blocked Shots	+2												+2
Free Throws Made	+1												+1
Loose Ball Recovery	+1												+1
Screen/Basket	+1												+1
Hustle	+1												+1
Deflection	+1												+1
Scoring Area Pass Made	+1												+1
Transition Pass Ahead	+1												+1
Positive Points	+1												+1
Turnovers	-2												-2
Not Rotating f(c)	-1												-1
Missed Shots/first half	-1												-1
Missed Shots/second half	-1												-1
Missed Free Throw	-1												-1
Not Back on Defense	-1												-1
Scoring Area Pass Allowed	-1												-1
Deflected Pass	-1												-1
Beaten on Screen	-1												-1
Not Having Hands Up	-1												-1
Not Contesting Shot	-1												-1
Not Blocking Out	-1												-1
Not Overplaying	-1												-1
Influencing Cut Off	-1												-1
Not Going to the Boards	-1												-1
Not Helping Half-court	-1												-1
"O" Execution Lapse	-1												-1
No Ball Pressure	-1												-1
Defensive Lapse	-1												-1
Offensive Lapse	-1												-1
Negative Points	-1												-1
Game Totals													
Game #2													
Game #3													
CUMULATIVE TOTALS													

Scenes from Five-Star

Meet the Coaches

Bill Agronin has been the head women's coach at Niagara University since the 1991-92 season. He posted a 32-22 record and back-to-back winning seasons during his first tenure and led the Purple Eagles to a first- place MAAC regular-season finish in 1992-93. Following the 1992-93 campaign, he was named MAAC Coach of the Year. The Purple Eagles have been one of the top 25 teams in the nation in team grade-point average for the past three years under Agronin.

For the last 12 years, **Kevin L. Allen** has served as the head girls varsity coach at West Florence High School in Florence, South Carolina, and a counselor at the Five-Star camp for the last eight years. Allen has been teaching and coaching for 22 years and has recently earned his master's degree in sports sciences at the United States Sports Academy.

A 1991 graduate of St. Joseph's University with a bachelor's degree in accounting, **Cindy Anderson** is the seventh-youngest head coach in NCAA Division I basketball. She was in her first season as associate head coach and fourth season overall on the Loyola coaching staff before being named head coach in December 1998. In her first season as head coach, Anderson won 17 of 23 games (.739), including a seven-game winning streak at the end of the regular season and into the first round of the MAAC tournament.

Matt Brzycki is the Coordinator of Health Fitness, Strength and Conditioning Programs at Princeton University. He has authored three books, co-authored another and written more than 190 articles on strength and fitness for 34 different publications.

The head coach at Cleveland State University since 1995, **Duffy Burns** became the Vikings' second-winningest women's basketball coach in school history after only his third season there. He led the Vikes to their first winning campaign in 15 years during his fourth season with the team, and during his fifth, they finished fourth in the Midwestern Collegiate Conference with a record of 8-6. During his tenure he has not only improved the team's play on the court, but he has emphasized the importance of achieving in the classroom as well. The women's basketball team consistently maintains a GPA of 3.00 or better.

Eight members of the 1998 team were named to the CSU Athletic Academic Honor Roll and five were on the MCC Academic Honor Roll.

One of the country's most successful women's basketball coaches, **Royce Chadwick** of Stephen F. Austin State University has an impressive .848 (346-121) overall collegiate winning percentage and has served as a head coach at every level of women's basketball. One of the top collegiate recruiters in the country, Chadwick was named the Women's Basketball Coaches Association's National Coach of the Year in 1992. Chadwick has also been named the WJCAC Coach of the Year five consecutive seasons, the Texas Association of Basketball Coaches Coach of the Year in 1993, and was the Converse District Coach of the Year in 1994. In the 1996-97 season, Chadwick recorded his 300th career victory.

Assistant Coach **Kevin Chaney** has been at Solano Community College since 1994. His duties have included everything from administration to on-court instruction. He is the current NCAA Assistant Coaches Representative of JC/CC Women's Basketball in the Women's Basketball Coaches Association and a respected clinician.

Joe Ciampi has never had a losing season in 20 seasons at Auburn University or two at West Point. Even as nine years as a high school basketball coach, Ciampi always posted winning records. To say that the man is used to winning would be a major understatement. He was named National Coach of the Year in 1987, 1989 and 1993, and SEC Coach of the Year in 1985, 1988 and 1989.

Greg Collins is a varsity assistant coach with head coach Mina Todd at DuPont Manual High School in Louisville, Kentucky. Coach Collins, whose responsibilities include post player development, played a key role in the Lady Crimson's 2000 Regional championship and Kentucky State Tournament Final Four run. In 1998, he coached Manual's girls to an AAU state championship. Coach Collins previously coached at North Bullitt High School (Shepherdsville, Kentucky), where he started a girls AAU program and in 1997 led them to their first National AAU Tournament. Coach Collins also teaches at the Five-Star camp every summer.

An international legend and multi-Hall of Famer in the game of basketball, University of Texas head coach **Jody Conradt** has established an enviable tradition of success. With her collegiate coaching accomplishments elevating her to one of the best all time, Conradt enters her 25th season at Texas and her 32nd year overall as a collegiate head coach, and ranks as the all-time winningest women's basketball coach in history with more than 725 victories. Conradt's long-term commitment to sport has been recognized as a key factor in elevating women's basketball into the national spotlight. Six times Conradt has been honored by her peers and the media as the National Coach of the Year, including her 1996-1997 selection as the John and Nellie Wooden National Coach of the Year Award in its inaugural year. Five times she was selected Southwest Conference Coach of the Year. In 1987, she received the Carol Eckman Award.

The new head coach at Oglethorpe University in Atlanta, Georgia, **Kathy Warner Corbett** played college basketball for four years and graduated from Rollins College in Orlando, Florida. She has served as an assistant coach at both Furman University in Greenville, South Carolina, (where she also earned her master's degree), and Wright State University in Dayton, Ohio.

Hired by Purdue on April 2, 1999, **Kristy Curry** was first blessed by being born into a coaching family. Her grandfather, Major Sims, was a teacher and coach for 41 years. Her father, Blake Sims, coached football in the prep ranks, and her mother, Ann Sims, coached girls basketball for 26 years. Curry, the first coach in NCAA women's basketball history to inherit a national champion team, made an impact in her first year with the Boilermakers. Despite beginning the 1999-2000 season ranked 23rd by the Associated Press (the lowest ever ranking for a defending NCAA champion), Curry engineered an impressive season by leading the Old Gold and Black to a 23-8 record (11-5 Big Ten), a third consecutive Big Ten Tournament championship, a top 16 seed in the NCAA Tournament and a final national ranking of 13th in the AP poll. Meanwhile, Curry and her staff inked the top recruiting class in the country according to the All-Star Girls Report. Curry came to Purdue following three years as an assistant coach at Louisiana Tech under the legendary Leon Barmore.

Charlene Curtis has been the head coach at Wake Forest since 1997. She came to the Demon Deacons from the University of Connecticut, where she served as an assistant coach for two seasons under head coach Geno Auriemma. In that time, Curtis helped lead the Huskies to a combined 67-5 record and two Big East Conference championships. Her coaching resume also includes a wealth of international experience. She was an assistant coach with the USA Basketball team that won a gold medal at the 1994 Goodwill Games, a bronze at the 1994 World Championships and a gold at the 1991 World University Games. She was a also a floor coach for the USA Basketball Olympic Trials in 1992.

A four-year letter winner and two-year captain at Aquinas College, University of Buffalo coach **Cheryl Dozier**, "CD," was an assistant for three different schools before taking the helm at UB, including a five-year stint at Michigan State, where she helped the Spartans win a Big Ten Championship and reach the NCAA's twice. In her first year as a head coach, Dozier led the Bulls to a sixth-place finish in their first season in the conference, after being picked to finish dead last. Coach Dozier is a member of the Women's Basketball Coaches Association, serves on WBCA committees and is an active member of the Basketball Coaches Associations of New York and Michigan.

In 15 years as a head coach, **Bob Foley** has amassed a career record of 251-182. His 1999 University of Richmond Spiders finished second in the regular season CAA standings and posted a school-record 11 conference victories. Prior to his arrival at UR, he served 11 seasons as head coach at Providence College. During his tenure, Foley amassed a record of 206-127 and is the all-time winningest women's basketball coach in Providence College history. While at Providence, Foley's squads made five NCAA Tournaments, one WNIT appearance, and won three Big East titles. His 1990 team finished 27-5 and 11th in the *USA Today* poll while his 1991 squad finished 26-6 (16th AP) and set an NCAA record, averaging 96.7 points per game.

David Glass begins his fourth season with the Virginia Commonwealth women's basketball program. In three years at the helm, Glass has led the Rams to three appearances in the Colonial Athletic Association tournament semifinals. For the past two seasons, Virginia Commonwealth has finished in the top five of the conference. Glass returned to Virginia Commonwealth in 1996 after serving as the head coach at the University of Missouri-Kansas City from 1993-96.

A veteran coach within the Lady Monarchs program, **Allison Greene** is entering her tenth season on the staff. At. Old Dominion, Greene serves as the recruiting coordinator with the primary responsibility of organizing all on and off-campus recruiting efforts for the Lady Monarchs. She will also work with head coach Wendy Larry on team scheduling. Greene's on-court duties include assisting with the development of post players and sharing the responsibility for the scouting of opponents. Greene is a 1990 graduate of Dartmouth College, where she holds several records for her outstanding play for the Big Green.

Karen Hall is the head coach at North Carolina Agricultural and Technical State University. In 1994 Hall was hired by Chatham College in Pittsburgh to initiate, develop and be head coach of the school's first NCAA women's basketball program. Hall, who played basketball collegiately at the University of Nevada-Las Vegas, served as an assistant coach at Cleveland State (1992-93) and at Duquesne (1989-91). An All-Pacific Coast Athletic Association performer and two-time team captain while at UNLV, she became the first woman to play and coach in the Connie Hawkins Men's Summer League and was the first woman to coach at Five-Star national boys summer basketball camp.

Since coming to the University of North Carolina at Chapel Hill in 1986, **Sylvia Hatchell** has posted a record of 269-133 and forged a tradition of excellence. Under her direction, the Tar Heels have won a national championship, four of the last six ACC titles, compiled back-to-back 30-win seasons, and claimed four ACC Player of the Year and three ACC Rookie of the Year honors. With a 33-2 record in 1993-94 and a 30-5 record in 1994-95, Hatchell became the first UNC basketball coach, men's or women's, to post back-to-back 30-win seasons. In 1994, Hatchell was named the National Coach of the Year by *USA Today* and *College Sports* Magazine. In 1996-97, she was named ACC Coach of the Year after guiding the Tar Heels to a 15-1 conference record and their first regular-season ACC title. Hatchell's stints in international competition also include serving as an assistant coach for the U.S. World University Games team that won the gold medal in 1983 and the team that won a silver medal in 1985. She was a court coach at the U.S. Olympic basketball tryouts in both 1984 and 1992 and also worked on the Olympic Games basketball events staff in Los Angeles in 1984.

When speaking about **Keith Holubesko**, the word "teacher" is the first thing that comes to mind. Priding himself on his ability to create the perfect drill for any skill situation, Coach Holubesko started his coaching career as an assistant girls' coach at Bridgewater State College in Massachusetts from 1994-97. In 1998, Coach Holubesko took over as head girls basketball coach at Rogers High School in Newport, Rhode Island. He has been part of the Five-Star family for the past three years, working both the girls' and boys' camps as a station master.

Recruiting is a major component for any successful college basketball program. The person in charge of bringing the best athletes to Saint Louis University women's basketball is **John Ishee**, who is in his first season as an assistant coach under Jill Pizotti. Ishee brought to the job 14 years experience coaching at the high school and collegiate levels. Having coached at nearly every level of the game, Ishee brings with him a vast knowledge of the game and a proven record in recruiting top-notch players.

Craig Kennedy began his coaching career at the age of 17. In 21 years of coaching he has coached from the elementary to the college level in both Canada and the United States. In July of 2000, Kennedy became the Director of Women's Basketball Operations at Auburn University under Joe Ciampi.

In May of 1996, **Nancy Lieberman-Cline** was inducted into the Naismith Memorial Basketball Hall of Fame, of which she is now only one of 16 women to earn such distinction. One year later, she came out of player retirement to play in the inaugural season of the WNBA, seeing action in 25 games for the Phoenix Mercury, which went on to compete in the 1997 WNBA playoffs. In November 1998, she was named to the inaugural class of inductees for the Women's Basketball Hall of Fame which opened its doors in June 1999. Lieberman-Cline is the 1999-2000 president of the Women's Sports Foundation (WSF) and in March of 1999 was named to the Kodak All-American Silver Anniversary team made up of the top 10 players in the history of Division I women's basketball.

Matt Masiero began his coaching career upon graduating from high school in the summer of 1990. He started by working numerous summer camps, such as UMass (Amherst), for Coach John Calipari, Mason-Dixon, for Coach Morgan Wooten, Berkshire Basketball Camp, for Coach Harry Sheehy and the famous Five-Star Basketball Camp, for Howard Garfinkel & Will Klein. He is currently the director of the Five-Star Women's Basketball Camp at Robert Morris College and co-director of the Backcourt Camp. He is also a teacher at Jeremiah E. Burke HS, in Dorchester, MA, where he voluntarily assists with the girls' team. He spends his winters scouting for both the Men's & Women's College teams in the both the Northeast-10 & Little East Conferences.

A.C. McCullers, the third-winningest girls basketball coach in Georgia after a legendary career at Morrow High School, is the fourth head women's basketball coach in Clayton College & State University history. The must successful coach in Clayton County history, McCullers compiled a career record of 648-157, a winning percentage of .803, and won 535 games at Morrow before announcing his retirement in the spring of 1999. He led the Lady Mustangs to Class AAAA state championships in 1989, 1990, 1991 and 1993 and had nine players sign with NCAA Division I programs since 1990. In 25 years, McCullers guided Morrow to 19 state tournament appearances, 12 regional championships and nine trips to the Final Four, including his last season.

Joe McKeown came to George Washington University in mid-September of 1989, inheriting a team that went 9-19 a year earlier. In just 14 months, McKeown had built the Colonials into one of the elite programs in the country. His first team improved five games, to a 14-14 record, and the program has soared past the .500 mark since then. In 1991, he was named an "All-American Coach" by the American Women's Sports Federation after being chosen the Atlantic 10 Coach of the Year. McKeown has also produced winning teams off the court, in the classroom. His philosophy of the student-athlete balance has made well-rounded people out of the players he has coached. During McKeown's tenure, the Colonials have not only produced All-Conference winners on the court, but Academic All-America and Academic All-Conference winners in the classroom. Under McKeown's tutelage, the Colonials have received Atlantic 10 Academic All-Conference recognition 14 times.

Coach **Amy Meehan** has served as varsity girls' basketball coach at Drury High School, North Adams, Massachusetts for the past seven years. During her tenure, the Lady Devils have won four divisional titles and appeared in post-season Western Massachusetts play six of the seven years. In addition to working at the Five-Star Girls' Basketball camp, Coach Meehan has run her own local basketball camp called "Big Shot" for the past three years. Meehan also serves as the Varsity Girls' Soccer Coach and a Social Studies teacher at Drury High School.

A 1986 graduate of Northern Illinois University, **Jack Miller** is entering his second season as Assistant Coach and Recruiting Coordinator at Rider University, in Lawrenceville, NJ. Before arriving at Rider, Miller was an assistant coach at Monmouth University from 1991-1999 and served as an assistant at Seton Hall University. Before entering the college ranks, Miller was the head girls basketball coach at Elgin St. Edward high school. In his first season, he led the Lady Wave to a 25-7 record and a 4th place finish in the 1991 Illinois Class A State Tournament. Miller has been teaching and coaching for the past 15 years and received his Masters in Education in 1994.

Dave Odom, who has guided Wake Forest to nine consecutive post-season appearances, including seven straight NCAA Tournament trips from 1991 through 1997, and Atlantic Coast Conference championships in 1995 and 1996, is recognized as one of the premier collegiate basketball coaches in America. Three times he has been chosen district coach of the year by the U.S. Basketball Writers Association and twice he has been a National Association of Basketball Coaches award-winner on the district level as well. The Touchdown Club of

Columbus (O.) also named him its 1995 national coach-of-the-year after conducting a poll of head coaches across the country. Also, Coach Odom has been the director of the Five-Star Women's Camps for many years.

Just finishing her first season as head coach at Ball State University, **Brenda Oldfield** spent the four years previous as the recruiting coordinator at Iowa State. Oldfield helped the Cyclones to a fourth-straight winning season with a 25-8 overall record and third-straight appearance in the NCAA Tournament in 1999. During her four years with ISU, the Cyclones compiled an 84-38 record (.688 winning percentage) and broke the single-season attendance record on numerous occasions.

Belinda "Boe" Pearman spent the two seasons before coming to Rhode Island with the American Basketball League's most popular franchise, the New England Blizzard, first as an assistant then as associate head coach. Pearman's innovative schemes allowed the Blizzard, who led the ABL in attendance in her two seasons, to evolve from a league doormat to a very competitive squad. In Pearman's final season, New England climbed out of the Eastern Division's cellar to a second-place finish and into the playoffs. Thirteen games into the 1998-99 campaign, the ABL disbanded.

A veteran of 15 years in the collegiate ranks as a player, assistant coach and head coach, **Jill Pizzotti** enters her sixth season at the helm at Saint Louis University and has the Billikens poised to take the next step up in competition. Pizzotti came to Saint Louis University from Indiana University, where she served as assistant coach for three seasons. She was the Hoosiers' recruiting coordinator and worked closely with Indiana's post players. Pizzotti has compiled 45 wins in fours seasons after taking over a program that hadn't won that many in the previous eight seasons combined. She has a 45-64 mark at the university in her first collegiate head coaching position. Pizzotti is already the second-winningest coach in school history.

Hired in 1997 to be head coach at Manhattanville College, **Stephen Post** has the benefit of more than 20 years of coaching experience. He has won three New York City high school championships and three New York City High School Coach of the Year awards. He has also served as an assistant coach at Division I Iona and Manhattan Colleges. This year he took the team to the state tournament for the first time since 1986.

As **Cheryl Reeve** enters her fifth season at Indiana State University, she can look back at the past several years with must enthusiasm for the future. Last season, ISU finished 18-11, fourth in the MVC and was invited to play in the WNIT, the first post-season appearance for the Sycamores since 1977-78. The year before Indiana State finished its best record in nearly a decade as the Sycamores went 17-11 and placed fourth in the MVC.

Since the day she signed scholarship papers to play basketball at Ole Miss, University of Florida coach **J. Carol Ross** has spent 20 years both creating and soaking up the traditions of arguably the finest women's basketball conference in the country. As a player at Ole Miss in the early 1980s, she was a member of the inaugural SEC All-Tournament Team. As a seven-year assistant coach at Auburn, Ross reached the NCAA championship game in each of her last three seasons – 1988, '89 and '90. Ross is Florida's all-time winningest coach, compiling a 184-91 record (66.9 winning percentage) in her first 10 years at the school.

Head women's basketball coach at SUNY Potsdam since 1999, **Nelson Schorr** was previously the assistant coach at SUNY Potsdam (1998-99) and Indian River (1995-98). Schorr is also the director of the Nelson Schorr 3-on-3 Charity Tournament and the basketball director at Camp Chen-A-Wanda. He has served a lecturer at numerous camps and clinics throughout the Northeast.

Coach **Tom Shirley** has been with Philadelphia University for 11 seasons and has a winning percentage of 73 percent (244 wins/90 losses) there. At the beginning of the 1999-2000 season he was ranked 19th in all-time winning percentage at the Division II level of women's basketball and is the all-time winningest coach at Philadelphia University. For the past nine seasons, Head Coach Tom Shirley's teams have won at least 20 games while advancing to the post-season in the last eight.

Jessica Smith is in her second year at Bishop Hartley High School in Columbus, Ohio. She has led Hartley to a 47-4 record and a state championship. In 2000, Coach Smith was honored as the Ohio Coach of the Year by the Associated Press, the District 10 Coaches Association and the *Columbus Dispatch*. Smith was a former college assistant coach at Fordham University and her alma mater the University of Rhode Island.

Bob Starkman is the head women's basketball coach at Broward Community College in Ft. Lauderdale, Florida. Prior to coach at Broward, Starkman was the assistant coach with the Eastern Regional Basketball Association's Brooklyn Beasts.

Eric Stratman has been coaching in Quincy, Illinois, for the last six years. He won a eighth-grade girls' state championship before moving to the position of varsity girls' basketball coach at Quincy Senior High School in 1999. Stratman's team went 18-8 and he was named IBCA District 17 Coach of the Year. He and his wife Julie have a son, Alexander.

Debbie Taneyhill became the first CAA women's basketball player to advance to head coach at the same institution. At age 29, the head coach at George Mason University is also currently the youngest head women's basketball coach in Division I. Upon taking over the helm of the Patriots, Taneyhill promptly led her squad to three straight victories over Maryland-Eastern Shore, UNC Wilmington and East Carolina. George Mason would then go on to sweep series with UNCW, ECU and William & Mary. Last season Taneyhill guided Mason to series sweeps over American, UNCW and VCU. Twice during the season they put together a string of three consecutive victories.

After coaching the Albany College of Pharmacy's women's soccer team for five seasons (1991-1995) with a 41-23-2 record, **Tom Weaver** took over the helm of the Lady Panther basketball team. Tom has also been the college's assistant director of Computer Services since 1988.

Debra Wein, M.S., R.D. is the president and co-founder of The Sensible Nutrition Connection (www.sensiblenutrition.com), a consulting firm providing nutrition services to universities, corporate wellness programs, health clubs and other organizations. Debra is a contributing editor for IDEA's *Personal Trainer* and *Health and Fitness Source* magazines serving fitness and exercise professionals. She writes regularly for *Men's Health* magazine and has published articles in *Marie Clare, Women's Sports and Fitness* and *Muscle and Fitness*. She has also been quoted in publications such as *Shape, Self, Allure and Prevention*. Debra has been featured on a number of occasions on the Fox 25 (WFXT-Boston) 10 o'clock news talking about soy, men's health, weight loss and many other nutrition and fitness-related topics. Debra has over 10 years of experience managing leading university fitness centers in New York and Boston. Debra is the author of *SNaC Pack: The Health Professional's Guide to Nutrition*.

One of the most admired and respected coaches on the international and collegiate basketball scene, Coach **Kay Yow** has amassed over 500 wins in her 24 years at the helm of the North Carolina State women's basketball program. Yow's squads have won four Atlantic Coach Conference championships and appeared in post-season tournaments 18 times. In 15 of the last 23 seasons, Wolfpack teams have won more than 20 games and appeared in the final Associated Press Top 20 poll. During her illustrious career, Yow has worked with two United States Olympic Teams and seven other U.S. select teams, including Pan American, World University, and World Championship squads. In 1988, she guided the U.S. Olympic Team to a gold medal. Yow has received numerous awards and accolades such as the prestigious Carol Eckman Award, whose recipient is selected by members of the Women's Basketball Coaches Association. The award is presented to an active coach who best demonstrates sportsmanship, honesty, courage, ethical behavior, dedication to purpose and a commitment to the student athlete.

About the Editor

One of the most successful head coaches in college basketball, Stephanie V. Gaitley has continued to elevate the St. Joseph's University women's basketball program into the national spotlight. The 1999-2000 season was a memorable one for Gaitley, as she won the 300th game of her illustrious coaching career. Additionally, she helped guide her team to its 13th Big Five title and 11th NCAA Tournament appearance. The 1999-2000 squad posted the program's 20th consecutive winning season with a 25-6 overall record.

Gaitley took over the Hawks' helm on June 20, 1991, and has guided SJU in the right direction from day one. In the nine years since her return to the Philadelphia area, she has posted a 186-81 overall record, 105-37 in the Atlantic 10 and 31-5 in the Philadelphia Big Five. She has also won two Atlantic 10 championships, seven Big Five titles, and led the Hawks to five 20-win seasons and five appearances in the NCAA Tournament.

Gaitley has been rewarded for her successes on the court. She was named the Big Five Coach of the Year following the 1998-99, 1996-97, 1993-94 and 1992-93 seasons. In November of 1995, Gaitley was honored as the March of Dimes Coach of the Year for the 1995-96 season, beating out all Philadelphia area coaches in both the collegiate and professional ranks. She was selected by USA Basketball to serve as an assistant coach for the R. William Jones Cup Team in summer 2000 where they took the gold medal. In the summer of 1995, Gaitley coached the West team to the Silver Medal at the U.S. Olympic Festival held in Denver, Colorado.

Gaitley's husband Frank has been an assistant coach for fifteen years. Stephanie and Frank have three sons, Dutch (13); D.C. (7) and Jordan Cooper (2).

Index